PHILOSOPHY FOR POLAR EXPLORERS

Erling Kagge

VIKING

an imprint of

PENGUIN BOOKS

VIKING

UK | USA | Canada | Ireland | Australia
India | New Zealand | South Africa

Viking is part of the Penguin Random House group of companies
whose addresses can be found at global.penguinrandomhouse.com.

First published in Norwegian as *Als jeg ikke lærte på skolen*
by Kagge Forlag AS 2005
First published in English by Pushkin Press 2006
This edition published by Viking 2019
001

Copyright © Kagge Forlag AS, 2005, 2006, 2019

English translation: Kenneth Steven
Foreword translation: Diane Oatley

Set in 9.7/15.5pt Malabar LT Pro
Typeset by Jouve (UK), Milton Keynes
Printed in China by Toppan Leefung Printing Ltd
Colour reproduction by AltaImage, London

A CIP catalogue record for this book is available from the British Library

ISBN: 978–0–241–40486–7

www.greenpenguin.co.uk

For Ingrid, Solveig and Nor

The Snow Globe, Ceal Floyer

Contents

Foreword:
Ground Yourself in Nature

When I am feeling cold beneath the open sky, there's an easy way to warm up: I pull the hood of my anorak over my head, draw the zipper up to my throat and pick up my pace. When my body heat returns, first in my torso and then down my arms to my wrists and finally underneath my fingernails, I can stop. Then I take out a mandarin, peel it and slowly suck out the juice by pressing each section gently against the roof of my mouth with my tongue.

Suddenly I feel connected: connected with the person who planted the tree, with the water the tree has drunk through its roots, the earth that cushions these roots, the branch that has carried the mandarin from fertilization to fruition, and the sun that has helped to ripen it. And I feel grateful. Grateful for being warm again and for the feeling of being in contact with the rhythms of nature.

At other times when I'm out on a walk, it's as if I'm not thinking at all. At any rate, I seldom notice any activity along the way. My mind goes into hibernation, and only very occasionally a solitary observation will cross it: how the snowflakes beneath my skis are created by a tiny drop of water, ten or twenty kilometres above the Earth's surface, becoming, piece by piece, a six-sided prism, consisting of 90 per cent air. How it then floats down through the atmosphere and lands on the ground in front of me. No two snowflakes are alike and none follow the same route. They are often, though not always, symmetrical. Until my skis compress them, that is.

Nature has its own language, experiences and consciousness. It tells us where we come from and what we should do on the road ahead. I grew up without a television or a car (my father considered both to be dangerously unhealthy) and spent a lot of my free time in the forest, by the sea and in the mountains,

so I have been spoon-fed with this knowledge.
Today, when we are expected to be available at all
times, grounding yourself in nature can be hard.
I forget about it myself sometimes, and when I look
around I get the feeling that many people forget about
it all the time.

The more I remove myself from nature and the
more I increase my availability to the modern
world, the more restless I become. The more
unhappy, too. I am no scientist and realize that
I may be mistaken, but my experience has been
that feelings of insecurity, loneliness and depression
to a large extent stem from the flattening of the
world that occurs when we are alienated from nature.
There is, of course, much to be said in favour of
man-made environments and new technology, but
our eyes, nose, ears, tongue, skin, brain, hands and
feet were not created for choosing the road of least
resistance. Mother Earth is 4.54 billion years old, so it
seems to me arrogant when we don't listen to nature
and instead blindly place our trust in human
invention.

In 2010 my fellow polar explorers, Børge Ousland from Norway and Haraldur Örn Ólafsson from Iceland, and I crossed Vatnajökull (also known as the Water Glacier), Iceland's largest glacier. We travelled light and carried everything we needed in the way of food and equipment on our respective pulks. By volume, Vatnajökull is the largest glacier in Europe. It is made up of 3,100 cubic kilometres of ice and covers 8,100 square kilometres of south-east Iceland. As is often the case with Icelandic glaciers, there are a number of volcanoes beneath the ice. While we were on our way across it, a volcanic eruption broke out in the neighbouring glacier, Eyjafjallajökull. Hundreds of people were immediately evacuated and the air traffic above a large part of Europe was suspended because of the clouds of volcanic ash. We were never in danger, but the experience made me aware of how a small volcano eruption in a remote region of Iceland can have huge consequences for an entire continent. Large volcanic eruptions can change the whole world. I sometimes wonder if we need natural disasters like these to remind us of the Earth's rhythms and forces. I'd like to think

that's not the case, or at least that we can choose to reconnect with nature from time to time in a more peaceful way.

During the first twelve years of my life my parents sent me outdoors in all kinds of weather. I believe I liked it, but then I grew bored with it in my early teens. I began putting my energy into indoor activities and partying instead. Seven or eight years later I started yearning for nature again. I missed the forest, the mountains and the ocean, the feeling of physical exertion in the outdoors. It was a yearning that came from inside me, a deep-felt need for close contact with elements not made by machines. To feel the sun, rain, cold, wind, mud and water on my body. To listen.

The Irish polar explorer Ernest Shackleton struggled longer and froze more than I have ever done, but I can identify with some of the thoughts he described towards the end of his life as an explorer: 'We had seen God in his splendours, heard the text that nature renders. We had reached the naked soul of man.'

Over the years I have begun to wonder more about the paths I have chosen, and those I have taken less consciously, to arrive at my current location. In thinking about this I found myself confronted with a series of questions which, I believe, most explorers grapple with at some point. Why push your endurance to breaking point? And why, with the pain of frostbite, blisters and hunger still fresh in your mind, would you choose to do it all again? Is there anything to learn from these experiences? I had no clear answers to these questions. So I decided to sit down and write in an effort to find them.

When I started writing this book many years ago I was most interested in everything hidden behind the horizon and not what was right in front of me. If I went out walking, I wanted to walk far and cover great distances. I had not yet discovered the pleasure of a short walk. Later, with teenage daughters, a demanding job and a new-found interest in art, I became aware that my life had gradually changed, and I directed my thoughts inwards. This resulted in two books – *Silence: In the Age of Noise* and *Walking: One Step at a Time* – both of which are, in different ways, about the silence we carry inside us.

Since then new experiences have brought with them new insights and perspectives. One of the things I have learned as an explorer is that, every so often along the journey, you have to stop and recalibrate, to take stock of unexpected events or changes in the weather. This book is a recalibration of sorts.

*

1.
SET YOUR OWN COMPASS

As a child if I could dream it or imagine it, then I could do it too. Everything that can be dreamed up between two ears is possible when one doesn't know any better. I could do everything I wanted: become a World Cup football player, sail around the globe, ski across the great wastes, climb mountains, live like Mohammad Ali, kiss the prettiest girl in the class, save the world from destruction, become a man like Albert Schweitzer, be a fireman, travel to the moon or to Mars.

As a child and in my youth I was never unique in any way. I wasn't particularly good at sport – I had to start one year late and was among the bottom three in the class for twelve consecutive years – and my circle of friends wasn't particularly large. I really didn't seem to have anything going for me. With buckteeth and thick lips, and speech and learning difficulties, I was an obvious target when it came to bullying. I never did anything extraordinary as a child. But I dreamed about it. And I didn't stop dreaming.

At some point it dawned on me that the chances of my being a fireman, a footballer, an astronaut and a superhero all at once were limited. My dreams became, it's fair to say, more focused.

In 1990, together with Børge Ousland, I became the first to reach the North Pole without the assistance of ski-doos, dogs or depots. In 1993 I became the first to walk alone to the South Pole – unlike most solo expeditions, I chose to have no contact with the outside world – and then in 1994 I climbed Mount Everest. In doing all of this, I fulfilled my ambition to become the first to reach the Earth's three poles. Without flying.

In this account I have written something of those dreams and ideas that never lost their hold on me. Dreams which evolve and which, in time, are brought to fruition by curiosity and personal ambition. How it's interesting to observe in myself that while on these journeys to my original goals, I began to set new ones . . . to see exciting possibilities and fresh horizons. I find it difficult to imagine this world without believing that most things are still to be done and experienced.

'I'd have done anything to experience what you did,' someone said to me after I made my first voyage across the Atlantic. I was twenty; we had just reached Barbados from Cape Verde off West Africa, and I had swum to land from the boat and put my feet on solid earth for the first time in a long two weeks. Over the years many have said the same to me. But I am not certain they really did want those experiences. Otherwise they would have tried.

When I was a kid, I was a great admirer of the Norwegian explorer Thor Heyerdahl. One of the first books I read was of his voyage in 1947 on the *Kon-Tiki* raft from Callao in Peru to the Tuamotu Islands in Polynesia. Heyerdahl had a fear of water after having twice almost drowned as a child; nonetheless he had a dream of crossing the Pacific on this handmade raft of balsa logs – which was a facsimile of the prehistoric Indian rafts they built in Peru. Six people sailed with the *Kon-Tiki* westwards for 101 days across the Pacific, in order to prove that this was how some of the settlement of Polynesia could have taken place.

I was hugely pleased and a little surprised when, in the autumn of 1994, I was invited to Heyerdahl's eightieth-birthday celebrations, and I looked forward to having the opportunity to pay my respects to him. At the party lots of Heyerdahl's old friends gave speeches. They all praised – as was fitting – this man who'd discovered so much, the *Kon-Tiki* man. Several of them, too, talked about the opportunities they'd had to travel with Heyerdahl, although for one reason or another – studies, partner, family, work – they'd been prevented from doing so. The speeches were long. Throughout them I watched Heyerdahl, who smiled to himself as he listened, and I came to a realization. 'The crucial difference between everyone else and you, Mr Heyerdahl,' I said to myself, 'is that you made your own choices and didn't let others make them for you. When you

had opportunities you took them, and thought about all the obstacles later.'

Had the speakers wanted their goal enough? Or had they instead chosen what seemed the safest option? Had they allowed others to make the decision for them? Or perhaps they considered the obligations at home weightier? The difference between Heyerdahl and the others seemed to be that Heyerdahl was following his own dream, while they were trying to follow the dreams of someone else.

Buridan's Donkey is the first philosophical puzzle I remember reading. It is about a donkey standing between two identical haystacks and illustrates what happens when there's a refusal to make a choice. The distance to each of the haystacks is precisely the same, and it's impossible for the donkey to decide which haystack to walk to and consume first. Time passes, the donkey weighs up the choice, never comes to a decision, and in the end dies of hunger midway between the two haystacks.

For me there's a great joy in setting targets. At the end of the day, they are my own. Not Heyerdahl's, not my neighbour's, nor those of my family. I'll do it! I'll sail across the Atlantic, help someone in need, buy a bottle of champagne, say no to a temptation, write a book like this, set up a publishing house, become a lawyer, start a family. The South Pole perhaps? Alone then to the South Pole! For me the decision was made the moment the idea came to mind. Thereafter all I had to do was think through in rational detail how it might be achieved. Had I turned things on their head – done the fine-tuning first, then nailed the idea, then thought it through to see if it was workable before deciding whether or not I'd pursue it – I'd scarcely have anything to write about in this book.

Now and again I wonder what has become of all the other dreams and ambitions that I never did anything with. I wonder where they are. I don't think I'd have to look very hard to find them. As many have noted before me, it's easier to take ourselves out of our dreams than to take our dreams out of us.

I don't recommend that anyone set out to do exactly what I have done, even though I know that many have it within their power. Those were my goals. My hope is that this little book will help you – irrespective of your age or gender – to find your own North Pole, your own Mount Everest, your own dream. It can feel both unpleasant and somewhat risky to change your own world. But perhaps it's even more risky to do nothing, and not to try to discover how good life can be.

What you will regret in times to come may be the chances you didn't take, the initiatives you didn't show. What you didn't do. If you say it's impossible and I say it's possible, we're probably both right.

*

2.

GET UP EARLY

Getting up at the right time in the morning is a polar explorer's greatest challenge. That's as true today as it was in the age of Ernest Shackleton, Roald Amundsen and Fridtjof Nansen. So when I'm asked what the hardest thing is out there on the ice, I'm never in any doubt as to my answer. There's something unspeakably tempting about remaining in one's sleeping bag when it's minus fifty degrees, as it was at times on our way to the North Pole. It beats crawling out of that sleeping bag and feeling as though you have been frozen up to your chin in ice, like a sinner in the Ninth Circle of Dante's Inferno. To save on weight Børge and I had neither sufficient fuel to heat the tent nor extra underwear, so for the sixty-three days and nights the expedition lasted I didn't undress once.

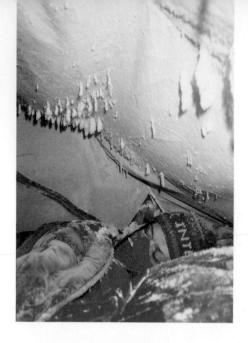

'This is the toughest thing I've done since my own birth,' Børge wrote in his diary. On that journey there was no shortage of reasons to remain in a sleeping bag: frostbite, illness, tiredness and injury. At low points we told each other that in the grand scheme of things this was a relatively short period of our lives, and that before long we'd be able to rest.

It was no different on the journey to the South Pole. 'There are certainly plenty who envy me, but few who would swap places with me,' I noted in my journal. The thought of getting up is far worse than the act itself in those situations. In that way it's like an Alfred Hitchcock film: there's no terror in the bang itself, only in the anticipation of it. Because the greatest danger is – as in a good horror film – putting things off. And get up I must. It's simply a question of whether I put it off for five minutes or five hours.

Getting out of one's sleeping bag isn't just the greatest challenge on an expedition, it's also the most crucial step. Most things are easy after that. It took many years before I ceased to be surprised that it was seldom as cold outside as it sounded when I was lying in my sleeping bag listening to the wind tugging at the flysheet of the tent or in the rigging. Roald Amundsen, the first man to reach the South Pole, wrote in his account that it was on the very days when the grounds for staying in the sleeping bag were most persuasive that things went best – once they got going. On expeditions, as in life generally, the final step is dependent on the first, and vice versa.

As an office worker and a father of three children,

it has struck me that the greatest challenge remains the same. It's about getting up at the right time, regardless of where I may be and what I did the evening before. So over time I've changed from being a late sleeper to an early riser as the demands on me have increased. This might not work for everyone, but it definitely works for me.

What I know of discipline I learned above the treeline (the highest point at which trees can still grow in the mountains). If it's cold, it's tempting to stop walking earlier than planned and if you're very hungry it's all too easy to nibble at a bit of tomorrow's ration. But there are few problems that disappear of their own accord. At home it's perhaps not so earth-shattering if I stay in bed or put off making an unpleasant telephone call. But out there I suffered immediate consequences when I procrastinated. For these reasons, I'm in no doubt that my experiences in the great outdoors have made me far more disciplined at home. Besides, the day is made so much better once the unpleasant things have been dealt with.

I have to admit though – before I come across as a moralist – that I don't always stick to my own rules. Even though I know what's best in theory and practice, I'm still to be found in my bed for too long now and again. And I still put off difficult or tedious tasks. It's exactly this freedom to make 'bad' choices that renders life enjoyable and challenging.

*

3.
TRAIN YOURSELF
IN OPTIMISM

A classic Zen Buddhist pilgrim's tale concerns the
wrestler O-nami, meaning 'Great Waves'. O-nami was
hugely strong and really knew the art of wrestling.
When he was practising he even got the better of his
own teacher, but when spectators were present he
became so shy that his own pupils could put him on the
mat. O-nami decided he would visit a Zen master and
ask for help. Hakiyu, a wandering teacher, had taken
up residence in a small temple close by, so O-nami
sought him out and explained his difficulties. 'Great
Waves is your name,' said the teacher, 'so stay here in
the temple tonight. Imagine you are waves. No longer
are you a fearful wrestler. You are the waves themselves
that sweep away all in their path, consume everything
in their way. Do this, and you will be the greatest

wrestler in the land.' The teacher withdrew. O-nami sat deep in thought and tried to imagine himself as waves. As the night sped by, the waves grew greater and greater. They swept the flowers from the vases. Even Buddha in his sanctuary was overwhelmed. Before the break of day that entire temple had become the ebb and flow of a veritable ocean. In the morning the teacher came and saw O-nami sitting meditating, the ghost of a smile on his lips. He patted the wrestler's shoulder. 'Nothing can disturb you now,' he said. 'You are waves. You will sweep away everything before you.' That very day, O-nami joined the wrestling bouts and won. Thereafter no one in Japan could defeat him.

The core of Zen is meditation. It's all about the power of thought. 'The struggle lies between the ears, not in the feet,' I wrote after the journey to the North Pole. If the body's able but we can't convince the head, it isn't easy to get anywhere.

I remember asking my daughter Nor, who was eight at the time, if she still believed she could achieve anything she wanted in life. 'Yes, but I think Solveig' – her younger sister of five – 'believes it even more than me,' she answered. I didn't quite know how to persuade Nor that nothing had changed . . . and that what she was being told are limitations which are best ignored for the time being. School, friends, the media, family and perhaps even I myself contribute unavoidably by saying over and over again that not all dreams can be fulfilled. Later in life, Nor will realize that she can't, after all, do everything she wants, but

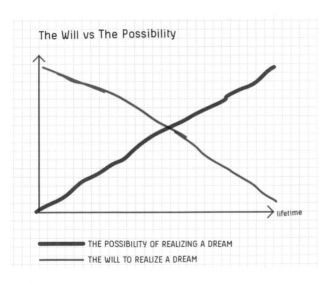

The Will vs The Possibility

lifetime

THE POSSIBILITY OF REALIZING A DREAM
THE WILL TO REALIZE A DREAM

I think it is better if that realization does not appear too early in life.

Naive optimism is something children seem to possess innately. In a child's mind the whole world remains unexplored; the world is changing, we are changing. I believe they are right. There is no finish line.

> *The best advice I ever got was from an elephant trainer in the jungle outside Bangalore. I was doing a hike through the jungle as a tourist. I saw these large elephants tethered to a small stake. I asked him: 'How can you keep such a large elephant tied to such a small stake?' He said: 'When the elephants are small, they try to pull out the stake and they fail. When they grow large, they never try to pull out the stake again.' Paul Vivek*

Put simply, optimism is a belief that the conditions of things can and will get better. Being optimistic obviously shouldn't mean being careless. Some might claim they are being optimistic when they take a chance on unsafe sex, reckless transactions, dangerous driving or walking to the North Pole without having taken necessary precautions. But that isn't optimism, that's stupidity. The American psychologist Martin Seligman advocates what he calls 'flexible optimism', which factors in risks, rather than blind belief in positive outcomes. When the cost of miscalculating threatens to be very severe, then it is time to be decidedly pessimistic in your estimation of how things will go. But when there's little to lose by being gung-ho and optimistic, then go for it.

If you are close to sinking in the middle of the Northern Atlantic, as my Norwegian friends Hauk Wahl and Arne Saugstad and I were, sailing back from the Caribbean in the winter of 1984, then telling yourself that there's no way to stop the water pouring into your boat is probably not going to help: you'll just give up. At the office I'm quite up for listening to and

considering objections, but seldom do I dwell on them unnecessarily. If there's something concrete that can be done to change the situation, then all well and good. If the retail price of a book we've published is too high, it's right to bring the price down. If I feel let down by someone or someone feels let down by me, I try to find out exactly what's gone wrong. Naturally enough, I may still feel sad and depressed as a result of criticism, but I dwell on it less today than in the past. I really do believe that it pays to try to have a positive attitude, and with a mental bat in hand whack away as much of the negativity as possible. If it doesn't disappear first time around, then you can always try again.

One of my first childhood heroes was the Englishman Daley Thompson, the world's best decathlon athlete for ten years. Thompson usually trained three times a day because he reckoned the other competitors would be content with twice, and that would put him ahead of the field. But it wasn't just his body he was training. He was also cultivating a mindset of self-belief informed by his physical exercise. On Christmas Day he was careful to train twice, in the event that one of the others would train that day too. 'If I trained twice, I would still know that I was up on them.' Most importantly, he believed defeats to be temporary setbacks: 'I'm good at it until proved otherwise.' According to Thompson he was competing first and foremost against himself, but he always trained harder than his competitors, and he knew in his own mind he was better prepared. Besides which, his competitors knew it too, which made them pessimistic. I wasn't all that old in the seventies when those battles between Thompson and his competitors raged, but it seemed almost predetermined that Thompson would win – if only by nothing more than a few hundredths of a second. And he did.

I am reminded of the Zen story of the great warrior Nobunaga, which emphasizes the importance of optimism. Nobunaga attacked an enemy force which outnumbered him ten to one. His odds weren't looking good. But Nobunaga turned to the spiritual world for help. He stopped at a Shinto sanctuary and told the troops that, after praying, 'I will toss a coin. If heads come up, we will win; if tails, we will lose. Destiny holds us in her hand.' He prayed silently, then tossed the coin. It came up heads, and his soldiers, inspired by the omen, crushed the enemy. 'No one can change the hand of destiny,' remarked his attendant sagaciously after the battle was won. 'Indeed not,' said Nobunaga, showing him the coin he had tossed. It was double-headed.

*

4.
DON'T FEAR YOUR
OWN GREATNESS

I've travelled to more than 100 countries and have met
quite a few people, and I'm in no doubt that the
majority of us undervalue ourselves. It seems that
many of us have a fear of our own greatness, and
so make ourselves less than we are. It's not always an
expressed fear, but an idea lurking in the background,
putting a damper on things. Almost like a little voice
inside each and every one of us saying that it's time to
give up, that it's not worth continuing, that we've
come far enough. It's easy to reject the exciting in
favour of the safe, and forget that we each have
numerous opportunities for new positive experiences,
and to achieve the things we've always dreamed of.
As Nick Cave sings, you got it, and you have to keep on
pushing, to 'Push the sky away'.

Greatness is relative. An acquaintance of mine is afraid of opening bills that arrive in the post. For him it would be an achievement to adapt to the world, to take control of things and avoid bankruptcy. Opening envelopes isn't normally about strength, but for him it is. What I have in mind when I talk about greatness is the potential of each and every individual to overcome obstacles. Small ones and, at times, great ones.

Another reason we may fear greatness is that the more we try to achieve, the more likely we are to put ourselves in situations where we risk failure. The fear of people's reactions if we fail is perhaps what makes us sweep our dreams under the carpet most frequently. It often feels safer not to try than to have a go and not succeed. When opportunities turn up at the door, it's easy to pull the blinds down and let them pass you by instead of following them and risking failure. I still remember sitting in the sauna after a skiing trip with a friend barely a year before we were due to leave for the North Pole. I asked him what he thought the public response would be if we were to fail. What would it mean for me? 'Don't give a damn about it!' was his immediate response. At the time I thought he was being a bit dismissive of what were, in my opinion, justifiable concerns. Later, once I'd thought it through, I began to see that with such worries I might as well plonk myself down on the sofa with the remote instead of going to the North Pole.

Sometimes people fear standing out from the crowd because they see it as tantamount to being lonely. I have read that a common reason for the collapse of a friendship circle is the greater professional success of one party, who then stands out from the rest in an unwelcome way. Generally it's the people who don't do so well who decide to cool the friendship or end it completely. Quite independently we can find the same conclusion in the title of one of Morrissey's older songs: 'We Hate It When Our Friends Become Successful'.

It's all right to be a little better, a bit more exciting – but not too much. Perhaps the fear of standing out from the crowd is something similar to the fear of being alone? If you become too different from the rest of the flock, it can be interpreted as treacherous and excluding. Part of the membership fee you pay to be part of a group is fitting in, and perhaps making yourself less distinctive so that your team members don't feel threatened.

It's easy too just to forget that there are other opportunities available to you than the ones which cross your path every day. For two years at the beginning of the 1990s I was a solicitor at Norsk Hydro, a leading Norwegian energy company. Immediately after starting I began to feel that the firm, or at least a large part of it, was dependent on me – that my activities were essential. A positive attitude certainly, but utterly crazy. To believe your work is terribly important is, according to the British philosopher Bertrand Russell, 'one of the symptoms of an approaching nervous breakdown'. At the same time I often felt dependent on my employer. Along with many of my colleagues, I imagined my workplace to be central to my world. I was deceiving myself and forgetting that I could choose another path. What is promised, in a promising career in corporate law, is of course more corporate law. Eventually I left to walk to the South Pole. My employer did better than ever the following year.

It is so easy to worship the wrong gods. I believe that most of us now and then benefit from at least considering the alternatives to the path prescribed by the industry we find ourselves in. Even if we decide that the path we are following is the right one for us, we will feel that we have decided it, it hasn't decided us. And sometimes we may uncover new opportunities which might otherwise have passed us by.

When I was fifteen I cycled from home in Oslo to Strömstad in Sweden to visit a girl I was in love with. It's a journey of about ninety miles and it took me half the day. I was standing outside her house – I still remember the address: Tallstigen 4 – stretching, when it suddenly hit me that I might just as well go home. Not bother to ring the doorbell. I was surprised at my own reaction. She was no less gorgeous than when I'd decided to cycle to visit her, but now that I was finally within sight of my objective, I completely lost the desire to go any further. Not because I felt the road itself had been the most significant element, but because I simply didn't dare to experience the next chapter. Since then I've encountered similar tendencies in people I have met: people who have been on the verge of attaining something, only to pull back. A friend finally got the job and salary he'd been striving for, and the opportunities for progression were great. But instead of going the full distance, he found he didn't give a damn; he couldn't or wouldn't go on.

In the Italian film *Cinema Paradiso* from 1988 an elderly man by the name of Alfredo tells the story of a soldier who was in love with a princess. He realized that a man of his standing had no chance at all, but he wouldn't give up all the same. One day the princess told him that if he stood outside her window for a hundred days and nights she would marry him. The soldier took up position outside her house. The days and weeks passed. He endured rain, wind, snow and cold. On the ninetieth day he could barely stand upright any longer, tears flowed down his cheeks, but he wouldn't give up. On the ninety-ninth day, when he had all but won his beloved, he gave up. Without further ado he just left. I saw that film with a friend. She reckoned he'd given up because he wouldn't be able to cope in the future with the humiliation of what the princess had put him through. A psychiatrist friend thought the soldier had walked away because finally he knew his goal was within reach, and there was no challenge any more. Perhaps so, but I can't help thinking that he left his place after almost 2,400 hours because he did not dare to remain in love – the greatest of all feelings – when the princess was no longer a distant dream. He was abandoning a future that was uncertain in preference for something predictable. This business of 'winning the princess and half the kingdom' – as the Norwegian folk tales have it – needn't necessarily be the start of a wonderful story. It's not automatically the case that one 'lives happily ever after'. Perhaps it's then the real problems begin, and the reason the fairy tales end where they do.

One of the major advantages of not fearing our own greatness is that we will cease to fear it in others. 'I could have done that too' is something I've thought many times when I've heard what others have done. Maybe, but I didn't. If I start bitterly thinking about all the reasons why that person isn't any better than me and shouldn't have achieved what I didn't, then all I do is let the small-minded side of myself get the better of me. Either I should have done whatever it was, or else I should simply think about it differently. Had I been smarter I'd have been happy with and for the person and thereby felt good myself, instead of embarrassed. Keeping small-mindedness at bay is an art, and the surest way to achieve it is by giving ourselves room to achieve and accepting that the achievements of others don't take away from that space.

I have a suspicion where at least some of these feelings that conspire to diminish us come from: most boys and men I know have a father complex. I know

I do. My father had a father complex, as did my grandfather and probably my great-grandfather. I believe many of our reactions to situations in our adult lives can be explained by the relationship – or lack thereof – between father and son. From the Old Testament and the return of the Prodigal Son to *The Lion King*, that father–son complex is a central theme.

I love my father deeply, despite the doubt he expressed about my abilities before and after every expedition. Other people could be negative too, but there's something about the terse comment – 'You will never make it', 'It's impossible' – made by a father. It cuts so much deeper. But even more than that, I can remember how much I wanted to please him. The first time I succeeded in that regard was when I returned from the South Pole. His praise meant more than any of the other accolades I received.

As I've grown older, I've come to realize that my father, like most other fathers, probably didn't mean any harm by his criticisms or rebukes. Often he just wanted to keep me safe, and he was probably justified a lot of the time: I wasn't always the easiest of sons. But with my daughters I have tried to be more of a 'can-do' than a 'can't-do' father. I know from my own experience that early criticism stays with us, and that the majority of us never quite rid ourselves of that anxious feeling which slipped in through the nursery door. If you're told as a child that you can't draw, it's easy to believe it to be true for the rest of your life.

What has most helped me to quash the little voice of negativity in my head has been to become aware of where it comes from, and that what it says is rarely worth paying attention to.

I don't mean that it's suddenly up to one and all to believe in their own greatness at the expense of self-reflection or realism. And by greatness, I don't mean superiority. I only believe it is important to think differently about yourself, sometimes, in order to unlock the door to doing what it is you want to do.

*

5.

DON'T MISTAKE PROBABILITY FOR POSSIBILITY

'We have to differentiate between what is completely impossible and what is merely improbable,' writes the Norwegian philosopher and mountaineer Arne Næss. Nothing is completely impossible, he insists – just less and less probable. All eventualities while you are alive exist on a kind of 'possibility meter' which goes from 0.1 to 99.9 per cent certainty.

On expeditions as well as in daily life I find Næss's logic very helpful. When I consider the history of polar exploration it is full of stories of people who survived against all the odds. On the night of 15 October 1882, for example, the American ship *Polaris* was hit by an iceberg off the north-west coast of Greenland. Nineteen of the survivors – including five

children – ended up stranded on an iceberg. They
landed there in one of the harshest, most windswept
corners of the globe, without adequate equipment or
sufficient sustenance. For six months they drifted on
the iceberg through the very coldest season of the
Arctic year. All told, they travelled some 3,000
kilometres south, from Smith Sound down past Baffin
Island and the entrance to Hudson Bay, eventually
ending up off the coast of Labrador on 30 April 1883.
I have travelled in the region myself, well equipped,
and for me it's still hard to comprehend that anyone
could survive for that many weeks on an iceberg with
such minimal provisions. Of course they came close to
drowning, freezing to death and starving; but they
built igloos and shelters for themselves from ice and
snow, and hunted seals. When they were eventually
rescued by a whaling crew, one of the sailors asked if
they'd actually spent the night on the iceberg. One of
the survivors described bursting out laughing for the
first time in months. People's immediate reaction was
one of incredulity, both that such a well-fitted ship as
Polaris could be wrecked in the first place, and that it

was possible that anyone could survive for half a year on an iceberg, without being in the least way prepared for the ordeal.

When Geir Randby (who had come up with the idea for the whole expedition, but who unfortunately was injured early on and had to pull out), Børge Ousland and I decided to walk to the North Pole, few believed we stood a chance. Perhaps, to begin with, it even seemed impossible to us, but from then on the probability that we would manage it began to rise in line with our preparations.

Before I travelled to the South Pole alone there were some who thought I was a touch mad, while others reckoned I would go mad on the journey. At school my teachers thought that because of my dyslexia and lack of concentration, writing a book would be an impossibility for me. As would, for that matter, having anything to do with a publishing house.

What is humanly possible changes, and we live in a time when most things are changing faster than ever before. Since the dawn of time human beings have viewed the wings of birds and had a dream to fly. It was impossible until the right materials and developments in physics presented themselves about a hundred years ago. According to the Royal Geographical Society, and to most of the others with an opinion on the subject, drifting right across the Arctic was an impossibility until Fridtjof Nansen and his men did so in the middle of the 1890s. Until recently it was considered impossible for a human to travel to Mars, but now it's only a matter of time before someone sets out on a journey of 33.9 million miles.

The American cult film *Dogtown and Z-Boys* recounts the history of the skateboarding fraternity in California in the 1970s, a small group of pioneers who subsequently turned the sport upside down by experimenting with what was possible with a skateboard. As Tony Alva, one of the film's participants, says at one point, they could envisage the moves they wanted to do, they just didn't know if it was possible to actually do them. The problem was that there was nowhere suitable for them to try out what they had choreographed. Then serendipity struck. In the course of one summer everything changed in a way that no one could have imagined. A great drought hit California and all the swimming pools quickly became bone-dry. Without asking the owners' permission, the gang from Dogtown laboriously set to work cleaning out these unused pools. With their solid surfaces and their sharp curves, they were perfect for skateboarding. So it was that Tony Alva, Jay Adams and their companions were finally able to put their ideas into practice, and thereby build the foundations of a global skateboard culture. What had been barely possible for a cluster of individuals to realize, all at once became something the masses could attempt.

There was a time when it was quite inconceivable that ordinary citizens could effect dramatic change by penning letters to leaders of states and generals across the globe. One day, the Englishman Peter Benenson was sitting on the Tube in London, wearing his bowler hat and carrying a copy of the *Daily Telegraph*. He had just been reading an article about two students in Portugal who had been imprisoned for expressing their beliefs, and it struck him that perhaps he should have a go at changing things. That was the beginning of Amnesty International.

A year later the organization was up and running and since then thousands have been helped. In 1975 the union employee Julio de Peña Valdez from the Dominican Republic was being held in custody. After the first 200 letters arrived on the prison's doorstep, he was given his clothes back. After receiving a further 200, the prison governor wanted to meet him. And after 3,000 letters had arrived, the country's president finally gave up and set him free. Today, Amnesty is the world's largest independent organization for human rights, and there's still much to be done in recalibrating what it's possible to achieve for freedom and justice.

It was considered impossible to climb Mount Everest without extra oxygen until the Austrian Peter Habeler and the South Tyrolean Reinhold Messner did so on 8 May 1978. Since they proved that it was possible, Messner has done it solo, and around 200 climbers have followed suit. Messner has also, together with the German Arved Fuchs, skied across

the Antarctic via the South Pole and flown to the North Pole. My point is that Habeler's and Messner's achievement was considered an impossibility until suddenly it wasn't. For any established but fallacious truth to be disproved, you need someone who can distinguish impossibility from improbability. So I'd recommend keeping in mind American Amelia Earhart's advice – she flew alone across the Atlantic in 1928: 'Never interrupt someone doing what you said couldn't be done.'

*

6.
DON'T TAKE STUPID RISKS

One thing most explorers have in common is this: that when we seek out challenges and dangers, it's not about playing with death – quite the opposite. We seek out danger because experiencing intense situations and having the ability to surmount them feel like a confirmation of our own power of existence.

I remember the last metres of Mount Everest. Just before you come to the absolute summit from the south-east side, there's a small sub-peak on the mountain itself. It's called the South Summit. From this and up to the summit proper the route goes along a very narrow ridge of ice and snow called the 'Cornice Traverse'. It's hellishly narrow and incredibly difficult to climb. To the left as you climb towards the summit, there's a steep descent of about 2,000 metres into Nepal. To the right side there's a sheer drop of about

3,000 metres into Tibet. With the exception of the odd small ledge, I reckon that nothing would break your fall before you landed in the bottom of the valley. One of the guys I was climbing with joked that he'd kept a bit to the left when crossing that perilous ridge, the reason being that, if he had fallen, the drop would have been a whole kilometre shorter than if he fell off the right side. I had a good laugh at that, but two days earlier, when – slowly and unsurely – I had climbed along that same treacherous ridge, I had thought only about getting safely to the other side.

Looking down from a great height has always bothered me. I grew no more fond of it climbing Everest, though I was slightly numb through lack of oxygen. I managed to get over certain elements of my fear in those weeks, but a good proportion of it remained. It was there the whole time. So as not to freak out completely, I simply didn't look down at points where it was steepest. The truth is, I didn't dare. Crossing the ridge I looked forward, meticulously watching the placing of each and every step. I wrote in my journal: 'Looking down to the right, and just a little to the left. Making up my mind not to do so again.' On those occasions when I did have to look straight down, I simply blocked out all thought of what could happen. I attempted with as much bravery as I could muster to fix my gaze and my mind on something else. In other words, I had sufficient courage to climb the mountain, but not to look down any more often than was strictly necessary.

Generally speaking it's not easy to be courageous; nor is it easy to know what is meant by courage. For me, at any rate, both are difficult concepts. Where does courage come from? Fear, a need for recognition, sheer folly or idealism? When my children jump down from high fences and trees, I think it's a combination of the latter three. Over the years I have thought a lot about courage and have concluded that it isn't a concrete quality that one is either born with or not. It's something that develops, something that is fostered or repressed at different times. Courage comes in different forms.

Being brave definitely means having some idea of the consequences of your undertaking. At home many thought we were courageous to set out on an expedition to the North Pole, not least because at times the temperature would drop below minus fifty degrees. When I travelled round South-East Asia giving lectures, I was met with little response when I quoted such temperatures; it didn't seem that fifty below meant anything at all to my Asian audience. It then occurred to me that perhaps they had never experienced the freezing cold and therefore weren't impressed by the idea of someone enduring temperatures like that. By contrast, it was because my listeners had seldom been alone for more than fifty minutes that they were so fascinated by the thought of being alone for fifty days on a solo journey to the poles.

Courage also doesn't mean carrying on regardless of the consequences, because to be reckless is not to be brave. It's no shame to turn back; that's rule number eight of the Norwegian Mountaineering Code. Now and again I've asked myself if one of the reasons why I've seldom turned back may be that I haven't had the courage to do so. It can be a jolly sight more tempting to expose oneself to extra danger than to be the object of disapproval or mockery. On my first expeditions I reckon that my fear of proving the naysayers right was at times an important motivation for going on. Since that time, now that my experience and intuition have become, one hopes, rather more developed, that fear factor has played a less significant role. Yet I happily admit that it is there now and again. The need for recognition has lessened through the years, but that doesn't mean it's vanished. When I climbed Everest, I was so exhausted during the last 300 metres that I went to sleep whenever I sat down on my rucksack to have a break. All common sense said that I should turn back. But, by that time, I'd stopped listening to reason. All I did was put one leg in front of the other, no matter the cost. I felt like an animal,

and I acted out of instinct and nothing more.
I've been given credit for my courage that day and for staying the course. Personally I believe I was neither brave nor cowardly, I was merely dopey and had stopped thinking rationally. Courage presupposes fear, or at least concern for one's safety, and that was something I had neither the wits nor the strength to consider.

The Swedish polar explorer Salomon August Andrée wanted to be the first to fly to the North Pole in his hot-air balloon, *The Eagle*, in 1897. The idea was to let himself be blown northwards from Spitsbergen by the southern wind. This was before the time of airships and planes, and Andrée was totally dependent on favourable wind and weather conditions. A short time before his departure he was informed that the wind between himself and the Pole was not blowing in the right direction, and that his attempt to fly would almost certainly fail. This was information that the Norwegian explorer Fridtjof Nansen could supply, having returned from a stay of some three years up on the Arctic Ocean (1893–6). With this information at his disposal, Andrée had to choose between returning home to abuse and derision, or embarking on the journey with *The Eagle* like a stubborn hero. He hadn't courage enough to return to Sweden, but he did have the guts to fly north – despite the strong risk of his dying. The corpses of Andrée and his men were not found until 1930, east of Spitsbergen, on White Island. To this day Andrée is considered a hero, and Swedish children are taught of his unrivalled courage. But, for me, the expedition's last man, the newly wed Nils Ekholm, is an even greater hero. This man chose to withdraw from the expedition when he realized that in all probability they weren't equipped for the task. He understood that in exposing himself to derision and scorn he was saving his new wife from the agony of grief, financial hardship and solitude.

A similar story can be found in *The Mystery of Courage* by the American author and professor of jurisprudence William Ian Miller. In 1914 an ordinary soldier by the name of Probert was commanded along with his American battalion to cross the

Atlantic to Europe to take up active service. The whole battalion had joined up as volunteers, but Private Probert refused to leave. When the colonel challenged him, Probert replied: 'I'm not afraid, Colonel, sir. But I don't want to be shot at. I have a wife and pigs at home.' His fellow soldiers made fun of him, and the colonel did his best to humiliate him too, at first beseeching him to change his mind, and then ordering him to do so. But Probert wouldn't budge. In the end the authorities gave up and he was dismissed from duty. The official reason given was not Probert's lack of willingness to risk his life, but his lack of intelligence. At any rate, the end of the story was that Probert 'went home happy and content to his wife and pigs'. Probert was comparable with Nils Ekholm, the man who withdrew from Andrée's journey by balloon to the North Pole – he was courageous in his own way. Perhaps he knew or guessed just how poorly the common soldier was treated in war, and how awful life was as a widow. In my eyes he displayed great courage.

When I returned home from Everest, Arne Næss said it was an impressive feat, but that it would have taken more courage to forget my ego, my single-minded desire to break a record, and instead to have turned around five metres below the summit, when I knew my goal was within reach. I do agree, but by then it was too late.

Some time back in Norway I spoke with a woman who worked as a prostitute in our capital. She told me how impressed she was that I had defied cold, wind and danger to reach my goals. This was on Christmas Eve, and I told her that in my eyes she displayed considerable courage in her daily existence. To trail through Oslo in a miniskirt when it was twenty below, and then jump into a stranger's car – and put herself into the hands of unknown men – that takes guts. We might have had different reasons for doing what we did – experience in my case, survival in hers – but in my eyes we both displayed courage along the way.

It was easier to be courageous when I climbed Everest and was in the public eye than when I did things completely unseen. Not that I wouldn't have climbed Everest if no one had been aware of my doing so, but it's undeniable that it's easier to show bravery when we can be sure of the reward.

I've taken some chances on expeditions. And at times it's been dangerous, when I've taken in sail on a rough sea, or sprinted across thin ice. At times I've been courageous; on other occasions, as I've said, I've barely been aware of what I was doing. In other moments too, as on the occasion when Børge and I were attacked by a starving polar bear close to the North Pole, we simply did what we had to in order to survive. Having to shoot a charging polar bear close up was a sad setback, but it was a question of who would have whom for dinner. I'm proud of what I've achieved, but when I think of it in terms of courage I feel I've perhaps been given more praise than I deserve.

Showing courage in day-to-day life can be a different challenge altogether. Now and again it strikes me that I'd rather climb Everest twice again than have to go through what some people face in everyday life, with

all its injustice and cruelty. Being responsible for raising three teenage girls seems far more daunting to me than scaling any mountain. It takes so much courage to battle a serious illness, to show kindness, keep promises, to end relationships – not to mention daring to love and to express love – to deal with betrayal, disappointments and sorrow. As the Norwegian psychiatrist Finn Skårderud once asked: 'What is a bungee jump compared to waiting for the call of a loved one that never comes?' An expedition lasts for several months; it's hard while it endures, but all those other everyday challenges last a lifetime. Give or take a bit. Conducting oneself properly in all of the myriad situations of normal existence, and being honest both with oneself and with others, is often tougher and a greater challenge than a journey where the whole thing will finish at a designated geographic point.

At times it's not easy to know whether greater courage is required to wait than to act. Emily Shackleton, Eva Nansen and Kathleen Scott were perhaps given no choice when their explorer husbands decided to put the ice before them, but they showed unsung courage when home and family had to be held together once the men had set off. When the husbands did not return, the authorities sometimes took care of the hero's family, but the majority were more or less left to fend for themselves. I reckon that remaining at home with sole responsibility for the family while the father was absent for several years (or perhaps for good) probably demanded greater courage than that which their men exhibited.

Although it isn't always easy to know what it is to be courageous, I reckon the majority of us recognize the feeling of courage when we experience it. Like Mufasa in the film *The Lion King*, I think I'm courageous when I have to be. Mufasa sees no point in exposing himself to unnecessary danger, he just lets that pass by. But when his son's life is threatened early in the film, he risks his own life to save him.

What is arguably an even greater challenge than showing courage for the sake of someone we love is showing courage when what has to be defended is not as close as the life or well-being of our nearest and dearest. For instance, plunging into deep, cold water to save someone we don't know from drowning, thereby putting our own life into real danger, and without anyone seeing us do so, is to display both physical and moral courage. I think I'd do it, but I can't be certain until faced with the situation.

The problem with courage is that it isn't something I can simply put in my Thermos and keep warm until the need arises, something that I can just gulp down like a few magic drops to render me brave and courageous. If it was, it would be something akin to the potion that gives strength to Asterix – a case of straightening one's back when the situation demands courage. The fact is courageous isn't something we are, it's something we become – just as cowardice is not bestowed upon us at birth. Being courageous is a new challenge each and every time the need arises.

*

7.

HAVE SOMETHING TO LOSE

Courage presupposes that the challenge has an
element of danger. It's great to work hard for a good
cause in the office of a charity, but courage is not
necessarily demanded. For any undertaking to be
truly challenging you have to stand to lose something.
This applies in great things as in small. You might be
risking the annoyance or scorn of others, physical
danger or economic uncertainty. When I was a kid,
I remember being impressed by a friend, a girl who
went against all the fashion trends at school in
choosing a highly idiosyncratic dress code all of her
own making, even though her parents were more
than willing to buy her what she needed. When
I think back on it now, I still feel it was quite
courageous on her part. Not to mention those who
were bullied and who, nevertheless, managed to

keep their heads above water and go to school day after day. When all is said and done, the individual who displays courage must risk something in doing so. And let's be clear about this – a position at work has to be given up, the face of a mountain climbed, a choice needs to be made at the expense of something or someone. If not, it may be something great, but it's not courageous.

Nowadays Norwegian society has so many inbuilt safety nets that the fight for survival is not the challenge it once was. Here in the West a steadily increasing number possess an ample sufficiency; the standard of living has never been higher, and dangers in general are far fewer. At the same time my impression is that a greater number feel they have less to live for.

My experience is that on those occasions when I, of my own volition, have risked something in my actions or my speech – chosen the narrow way – life has been given extra meaning. It's always risky to choose your own way, to gamble on what is uncertain. Health, kudos, self-image, money or life itself may be on the

roulette wheel. But not doing it can be dangerous too – duller also. Certainly, the dream of a danger-free and risk-free society is as old as humanity itself, and has much to commend it. Politicians in Norway endlessly discuss the possibility of creating it. I'm not saying we shouldn't strive to ensure as few accidents as possible happen in our day-to-day lives, but life without a little elected risk now and then is not much fun either.

Even if we take every step to guarantee our safety, accidents still happen. Most accidents happen at home, and that's if illness or reckless driving don't get you first. That applies to polar explorers as much as office workers. Danger is relative too. The mountaineer Tenzing Norgay, who with Edmund Hillary became the first to reach the summit of Everest in 1953, didn't die with his boots on in an accident on one of his innumerable climbs. He died of tobacco. Tenzing Norgay measured the situation so well as they neared the summit on 29 May at about 11.30 local time that he let Hillary pass him and walk six feet ahead just before they reached the goal. To be the very first was of greater importance for a white

New Zealander than for a sherpa, who felt perhaps that his people, in a spiritual sense, had been to the top many times already. Fridtjof Nansen, who in 1895 set the 'furthest north' record, died peacefully at home. It's fitting that, though he died at home, the last words he wrote in his diary were 'further and further north'. Reinhold Messner managed to climb and descend the fourteen world summits that rise over 8,000 metres, only to be badly hurt after having to climb a wall of his own home to an open window because he'd forgotten his keys. Short stages on the journey can be very dangerous and I've often felt civilized life can be just as treacherous as anything I've encountered in the great outdoors: like when I cycle through Oslo to my office, or when children cross the street alone, or when I'm waiting for a taxi late in the evening surrounded by drunk and aggressive people. And, besides, if you spend most of your life sitting on your sofa, your chances of heart disease increase.

Our lives will never be free from danger, either above or below the treeline, but when one gambles on one's chosen path, defying danger becomes a desire in itself. Without it, you may as well have gone by helicopter or snowmobile. Danger is minimized before and during an expedition, but if it's absent there's no gamble whatsoever.

I don't want to romanticize danger, but it puts me in the right frame of mind to weigh things up. It helps me get an overview beforehand of what could potentially go wrong and how I could contain the situation. By this process, I am able to determine in advance just how dangerous things are going to be. If I'm observant on the journey, I'll almost always find safer alternatives. Over time these dangers become part and parcel of daily living; one grows used to them and they become a natural part of one's existence. Without that little bit of uncertainty, I think I'd rather do something else instead.

Optional risk and danger are still, obviously, a luxury. At times, they can be extremely uncomfortable, but we are privileged to be able to afford them, irrespective of whether we are out in the wilds or somewhere else. In the old days the vast majority of people in Norway had enough of a battle just keeping body and soul together, for both themselves and their loved ones. I still remember my grandfather telling me of the brutal life he endured at the children's home where he grew up from the age of six. His mother couldn't afford to keep him at home after great-grandfather was washed overboard on the high seas. Daily life thereafter was a struggle for my grandfather: a fight for survival which for the most part meant obtaining food, clothing, somewhere to live and a smattering of education. I always thought of my grandfather as someone who had a great deal to live for.

With all due respect to those for whom daily life is a struggle, I believe that we humans have a need for challenges in the form of situations where we feel it's up to each and every one of us to earn the gift of life. At any rate, I for one need that. There are still mostly Stone Age genes in us. When dangers and challenges present themselves, I live in quite a different way; they

create meaning, and I feel fundamentally that I'm aware of being alive. Past and future are of no consequence. All that counts is my situation there and then. As for the other stuff . . . the dream of a lottery win, a better car than the neighbour's, or any ambitions that are the result of the influence of others – they no longer have much meaning. When a problem arises at the office and we have to think smartly and act fast, or when I cross Mount Everest's notorious Khumbu Glacier, or when I am hugged by my children, or when I sail in stormy weather across the ocean – I'm alive to my own existence.

8.

DON'T CHASE HAPPINESS, LET IT CHASE YOU

Have you ever asked yourself if you're happy? And wondered properly why you are happy? It's something I've done. And although I felt I was happy when I asked the question, I began to doubt the answer soon enough.

One of Aristotle's fundamental ideas is that human beings who want to live a good life must strive to develop their potential and to live in accordance with it. You must not strive for the wrong things, like wealth or fame. A good life is about using one's senses, seeking knowledge, living in fellowship with others, and being engaged in that striving. Contentment will come to one who is content, to put it simply. It's rather dangerous to take just a couple of ideas from Aristotle's *The Nicomachean Ethics*; yet it gives me great delight to do so because it reminds me that these fundamental thoughts and challenges remain the same throughout history, today just as much as 2,300 years ago.

When I've actively searched for happiness I've never found it. I don't deny that others can find one single absolute meaning for life, but I haven't managed it. In my experience the meaning of life changes from day to day, from year to year, and from person to person. The challenge for me, therefore, is to find purpose on life's different paths. I chose extreme journeys in desolate places. As Alex Honnold, the American solo climber, puts it: 'Nobody achieves anything great by being happy and cozy.'

Today I live a very different life to the one I did as an adventure seeker in many ways. There's a season for everything, and to live dangerously in a physical sense doesn't tempt me as once it did. Family life and exciting work provide me with a purpose I didn't have before in the day-to-day. Nonetheless, in order to live a fulfilled life, I constantly need to extend my boundaries, set myself tests. That life may be meaningful in all circumstances is something which, for me, is all too easy to forget. It's my choice. It doesn't always need to be something big. A short ski trip, caring for others, reading a good book, showing generosity, being together with my children, looking at art, talking to a stranger in the street – all of these things can give just as much joy and the feeling that life is meaningful as dangling from a rope below the world's highest summit. Now and again the latter can even appear meaningless in comparison with the rest. As many have noted before me, it's not about finding a single meaning for life, but about finding a variety of meanings in life . . . by paying attention to the day-to-day stuff, the moment-to-moment.

A great experience few explorers talk about, maybe because it is too obvious to them, is that life in general feels long when you – for a few hours, days or longer – live close to nature and slowly wear yourself out by putting one foot in front of the other many, many times. A lot of people I meet in Oslo and when I travel in urban areas view their lives as short, particularly as they get a bit older. I think that's a bit sad. To me they seem to confuse physics with their own perceptions. To feel the flow of time has less to do with the former than being an effect of our neural structure.

Two thousand years ago the philosopher Seneca wrote with wisdom on how time can be experienced on an emotional level: 'You are living as if destined to live for ever.' He goes on to describe how we humans live through other people, and are never centred in our own lives. We are careless with our own time. While we guard our property and social status as if they're the most important things in life, we have a completely casual attitude to our time, the one thing that we know for a fact to be finite. He who exists 'hustles his life along, and is troubled by a longing for the future and weariness of the present'. When they come to the end of it, 'the poor wretches realize too late that for all this time they have been preoccupied in doing nothing'. The nightmare scenario for Seneca is to die while doing your own accounts as your inheritors stand behind you enjoying themselves.

Seneca is, of course, making sweeping generalizations here, but I do agree with him that our lives will feel long enough if we don't throw away our time. It is about being present in the moment and living less through other people or technology.

It's only in recent years that science has managed to follow the development of feelings inside our heads. Our frontal lobe, an area right behind the forehead, plays a crucial role when decisions are made in a few hundredths of a second as to whether a certain situation is interpreted as appealing or not. Thereafter the signals are sent back, further under the scalp, to be worked on. Hundreds of millions of infinitesimally small connecting points in the head are connected to other nerve cells, and influenced by hormones controlling happiness, stress or optimism.

Both you and I are able to influence the interplay between positive and negative feelings, and thus the outcome. One of the breakthroughs came when researchers in September 2002 followed the minute-by-minute physical development in the brain of a Buddhist monk – which they measured using a cap fitted with 256 thin wires – who gradually worked his way into deep meditation and the feeling of happiness which characterizes this state. On the screen it was possible to see that parts of the brain lit up with electrical activity as the monk progressed inwards. It made clear, claimed American psychiatrist Richard Davidson, who was part of the research team, that happiness isn't a vague, indescribable feeling: 'it's a physical state of the brain', something you can induce deliberately.

In other words, scientists were in the process of proving what Buddhists practising meditation have known for centuries. Happiness is a state we can achieve ourselves, but that can have little to do with what goes on around us. Parts of the brain are in a constant state of flux, and we can reprogramme them if we choose to do so. The research team has, in addition to plotting the physical characteristics of the feelings of happiness, concluded that what they have seen happen in the brain – as most people who

have walked or climbed far have felt – also affects our body.

I sometimes try to figure out how happy the people I meet are. In December 2010 the American urban historian and explorer Steve Duncan and I descended into New York's mystical network of sewers, subways, train and water tunnels to cross from the northern Bronx to the Atlantic Ocean partly underground. Walking through Manhattan's West Side Tunnel, we visited Brooklyn, a woman who had lived in the tunnel since 1982. Her home was a concrete space twelve feet above the tracks which she called her 'igloo'. Her bed was a mattress on the floor, nicely made up. A pile of empty bottles and cans comprising the bulk of her possessions was in the corner. A magazine article with photos of Michael Jackson had been torn out and the pages hung side by side on the wall. She also had a photo of herself looking very beautiful.

I was curious about her thoughts on happiness. Steve and I had met Brooklyn on an earlier hike and we agreed she appeared more happy than most New

Yorkers we saw above ground. 'How happy are you, on a scale of one to ten?' I asked her. 'Seven,' she replied, and added, 'sometimes eight.' Brooklyn went on to explain that she is the most happy when she has finished emptying dumpsters up on the street for food, drink and clothing and returned to her igloo to be playing with her cats and feeding them. And also when she sings hits from the early eighties, around the time when she moved in. As she explained, 'It's called "appreciate what you got".'

I have put this question to many people throughout the world, and almost everyone answers about seven when they have to reply quickly. Once, when travelling east to Kamuli in Uganda with my daughters, we got to know a woman who lived with her husband, seven children and hens in a hut of about forty square feet. There were three beds in the hut, but no electricity or water, and there wasn't even a bucket to use as an outhouse. After thinking about my question, she also said seven, but then corrected her answer to closer to eight. Her husband stuck with his answer of seven. He had two wives and a total of seventeen children. There are two harvest seasons in Kamuli. The couple explained that after all their work, close to the harvests, especially if it proved to be a good year, a feeling of well-being came to them. During our three days in Kamuli, my youngest daughter, Ingrid, remarked that it was strange how people here were so much more cheerful than most Norwegians, even though we are so rich and they are so poor. In fact, if I ask almost any Norwegian – including myself – to rate their happiness on a scale of one to ten the answer is usually the same: seven, sometimes eight.

If I'd forgotten just how little can separate feeling happy from feeling down, I was certainly reminded of it on the way home from the Caribbean when I was twenty-one. I was in the company of two friends of the same age, Hauk Wahl and Arne Saugstad, when we hit seriously bad weather in our thirty-five-foot sailing boat just north of the Azores. The sails were torn to ribbons by the wind, the hatch in front of the mast was washed overboard, and the boat was on the brink of sinking. In such situations the best pump on the market is frightened boys with buckets, so together we managed to save that boat.

Under such circumstances one's mood changes more quickly than it normally would. First came desperation when the front hatch was washed overboard and the boat began taking in water, then there was the sheer delight when, against all the odds, we managed to find the hatch floating in the sea and so were able to rid our vessel of water. Then came pure bewilderment as a monstrous wave literally swept away the mainsail, a situation exacerbated by the fact we had no engine, the toilet was blocked, and the only cooking appliance was broken. We were living on raw corned beef, damp crackers and raw potatoes, and when we had to relieve ourselves we did it by hanging out from the boat. You can imagine our feeling of joy when finally we reached Brixham, a small fishing town in Devon in south-west England. For the first time in fifteen days after leaving the Azores we could again walk on solid ground, sit down and drink without being soaking wet and worried. The point is that all states – both positive and negative – will pass. With the negative ones, you often just have to ride them out.

'Either I'm happy or I'm not, that's all,' wrote the Austrian philosopher Ludwig Wittgenstein. His definition of happiness could well describe that voyage of ours home from the Caribbean. At one moment we felt in heaven, the next in hell.

A story about how nature has given us pain to our benefit is told of the Greek philosopher Socrates. He was arrested and put in chains. When finally the chains were loosened from his legs and he felt just how sore they had been, he reflected on how wonderful it was to be rid of them. Socrates was keenly aware of the relationship between pleasure and pain, and how those feelings complement each other, each eliciting and chasing the other in turn.

I've seldom felt a greater sense of well-being than I did on those occasions on my way to the North Pole when, despite the temperature sinking to fifty below and the food being the same day after day, I could lie down in the tent and feel the warmth flow into my body and could eat to dull my intense hunger. I knew then that Socrates was right. I was in no doubt that I was in fine fettle and eating the best cuisine I'd ever tasted. And still today I don't doubt that.

In *A Wanderer Plays on Muted Strings*, the Norwegian writer Knut Hamsun tells the story of a prisoner who's being taken to his place of execution. He's sitting on a cart and a nail is snagging his arse. It's painful, and the prisoner shifts position. At once he feels his situation to be more comfortable. Happy moments or good experiences – they are times we all have, Hamsun concludes.

Aristotle thought that a life had to be looked at holistically. If a person succeeds in realizing their potential, then they have had a happy life. The conclusion must wait, in other words, until the end. I have sympathy with this idea, both as an explorer and as a family man. You can only measure a thing like fulfilment by looking at the bigger picture. At the same time I like to stop in my tracks now and again, and just be content with the state of things. For instance, when warmth returns after freezing cold, when a daughter throws her arms round me with joy, when I watch a good football match – then life is good and I feel happy.

*

9.

LEARN TO BE ALONE

I've felt much more lonely in large gatherings of
people and in crowded towns than I did on my way to
the South Pole. Far out on the ice, 1,000 kilometres
from the rest of humanity, I hardly ever missed the
company of others. Now and again I missed skin-to-
skin contact, but seldom more than that. I had enough
in myself, my experience of nature, the rhythm and
forward progression of putting one leg in front of the
other a sufficient number of times. When I was alone
in New York for the first time, in the summer of 1986,
penniless and knowing no one, my sense of loneliness
was oppressive.

Having people crowding round can remind you just
how lonely you actually are. On the way to the South
Pole I had no contact with the world about me and
perhaps for that reason I missed human contact less.

It was a great relief that I couldn't communicate with anyone by radio or phone. To have had such contact would have resulted in some part of my consciousness never having left Norway, and I'd have missed out on a great deal of what the journey alone had to offer me.

I was reminded of the importance of being at the centre of my own life in the course of that journey. Of not living my life through others. Past and future merged into one another and became definitions of little meaning. There was only the present. No TV series, no adverts, no news, no celebrity gossip, no one else to consider. Just enormous white expanses all the way to the horizon. Sun and blue sky twenty-four hours a day (well, almost). A life such as that gives an enormous sense of freedom. The freedom to be alone, and the freedom to follow a dream.

'Loneliness is of course not an asset in and of itself. It often feels like a burden, but it also has potential. Everyone is lonely – some more than others – but no one escapes it,' writes the Norwegian philosopher Lars

Svendsen in his book *The Philosophy of Loneliness*.
Many religions and philosophical systems across the
ages have emphasized that loneliness can be
something positive, but today many people perceive it
as something intrinsically negative. For me it's all
about how I respond to the situation of being alone,
whether I'm able to harness loneliness in a good way
or whether I just become restless or a little frantic.
Often I find that I'm restless for the first hours and
days of a period of being by myself, but usually – if I can
stay the course and not allow myself to be tempted
into seeking out company or distracting myself by
thinking about the past or future – a sense of calm
settles over me after a time. Then I can start to enjoy
being alone. That experience of loneliness is very
close to what is sometimes termed 'solitude'.

When I was a child I didn't like being alone.
It was generally because no one wanted to play with
me and, as a result, I associated it with feeling down.
A feeling of security came from being in company –
preferably lots of people at the same time, and, best
of all, people of a similar age. I have fine memories of

playing ball games with friends in the neighbourhood. In many ways my life as a child was lived through others. To an extent this is normal. The need for togetherness and to have recognition from others is part of the human condition. Feeling that you haven't chosen to be alone but that isolation has been imposed on you is very different from electing to spend time by yourself. As a child, I had little notion of enjoying time on my own. On the way to the South Pole, and on other expeditions too, I began to wonder if I wanted that degree of social contact because I really yearned to be with people the whole time, or if it was really because I feared being alone.

The French philosopher and boredom theorist Blaise Pascal wrote in the seventeenth century of human beings' centrifugal force. We are willing to do almost anything it takes to avoid being reminded of our own meaninglessness in the world, and the way to do that most effectively is to be as busy as possible, so we don't have time to stop and reflect. Man, according to Pascal, is the only creature in the universe able to comprehend its own situation. I hadn't read Pascal when I went searching for the South Pole, but his description is very much in line with the realization I came to on the way: that my motivation for being so social was about running away from myself. And that realization felt crucial.

When I eventually reached the pole, I was asked if I'd learned much over the course of the journey. To that I emphatically said yes. The journalist then asked what it was I'd learned. To that I didn't have any simple answer. Not because I was in any doubt that those fifty days had been the most educational of my life, but because not all understanding can easily be expressed in words. And for me the journey had begun long before I came to the Antarctic and is still continuing. Today, several years later, I still don't have all the answers to what I learned during those days and nights on the ice. But I do recognize that it was during that period of my life that I learned that it was possible to live in a different way to how I had done before. Being alone, being left to oneself for an indefinite period of time, isn't dangerous. Quite the opposite.

When I came home my life continued as before. Invoices had to be paid, clothes had to be washed and when my washing machine broke down it had to be repaired. The difference was that I was more certain of what was important in my life. I became better at separating things that really meant something from what meant far less, and sorting out which people were of importance to me and which were not. I also knew that now and again I had to be alone, or else I could easily forget just who I was.

I've no intention of going back to Antarctica and spending the rest of my life there. I'm far too fond of family, friends, art, the sea, the woods and the mountains for that. If you ask almost any philosopher or thinker in history what they think about humans' need for company the answer will always be this: we are not made to be alone in life. We are mutually dependent on one another.

But it's good to know that I can endure my own company from time to time and to understand that occasional solitary periods do me a lot of good. They enable me to get away from the city, take some time to

[92]

reflect on challenges in my life, and, by realizing that I miss the company of family and friends, to appreciate what's important in it. I find that being alone makes me more curious about people – not just those who are close to me but strangers too – to listen to them, to respect them and to be interested in their troubles and their joys.

*

10.

ENJOY SMALL HELPINGS

Sometimes too much of what's good isn't good, it's simply too much.

'At home I enjoy large helpings. Down here I'm learning to value small pleasures. The subtle shades of the snow. The light wind. Cloud formations.' I wrote this in my journal on the way to the South Pole, on day twenty-two. In the course of three weeks I'd not seen or heard a single sign of life. No people, no animals, no aircraft. I'd put some 500 kilometres behind me and had more than 800 to go. When I began that journey I felt that everything round me was completely white and flat all the way to the horizon, and that above the horizon it was blue. But over time I'd started to see things differently. The snow and ice were no longer just white, but myriad shades of white, and contained glints of yellow, blue and green. I slowly began to see variations in the flatness – small formations which on closer inspection were like works of art, and different shades of colour worth focusing on.

'It's a clear day. The hugeness of the landscape and the colours of the snow make me happy. Flatness can be beautiful too, not just mountains. I used to think that blue is the colour of poetry, white of purity, red of passion, and green of hope. But here such classifications don't seem natural. Now all of them stand for poetry, purity, love and hope. And tomorrow blue and white might stand for storm and frost.'

Your experience of your surroundings can change dramatically over time, even if your surroundings don't change significantly. What alters is what's inside your head. 'What in truth is sublime must be sought in the mind of the judging subject, and not in those objects of nature which give rise to the mood,' wrote Immanuel Kant. He was not a philosopher known for his affinity with the natural world, but nevertheless he demonstrates a clear understanding of how to appreciate it here. What is beautiful lies in nature, but for our surroundings to be not just beautiful but truly sublime, a transformation has to occur between our own two ears rather than in what we see. What appeared as beautiful to me at the outset of my trek to the South Pole became in the fullness of time a sublime experience. It was all about noticing small details: a mountain on the horizon, the wind, a snow crystal, a formation in the ice.

The stillness in the Antarctic is more profound, and can be heard and felt more clearly than almost all sounds. Silence is eloquent. At home there's always a radio on, a phone buzzing, vibrating, or a car passing by. All in all there are so many sounds that I barely hear them. In the Antarctic, when there wasn't any wind, the stillness was far more powerful than back home. In my journal for day twenty-six I wrote: 'Here stillness is all-absorbing. I feel and hear it. In this endless landscape everything seems eternal and without limit. The soundless space does

not feel threatening or terrifying, but comforting.'
At home I barely notice what is happening
around me, but here I became so drawn into
my environment, so much a part of it, that stillness
became part of me, something I could listen to. If I
had enough energy for it, I made new discoveries
each day. I was completely isolated from anything
that lay beyond my horizon, so it was only my
nearest surroundings I could relate to. As the weeks
passed, my impressions of those surroundings
became stronger and stronger. Gradually I worked
up a dialogue with them, a dialogue that was
dependent on what I could contribute and what I was
able to take in. Not a conversation in the normal
sense of the word, but an exchange nonetheless
where I sent out thoughts and received ideas in
return. Towards the end of the journey, on New
Year's Eve, I wrote in my journal:

At the same time as I have felt my own smallness
in relation to the natural environment, I've also
felt an inner greatness. I've experienced terror

and joy, known relief and disappointment,
beauty and pain, have asked questions and found
some answers, sensed closeness to the elements,
given of myself and received, had the joy of
physical exertion, and been strengthened in the
view that there are still challenges and dreams
worth giving one's all for. Although the great
truths have not been revealed, I can understand
that time in the desert was decisively important
for great leaders like Jesus and Buddha. Here one
may experience what one cannot elsewhere.

When I think back it's that closeness to the natural
environment which made the greatest impression
over those fifty days I was alone in the Antarctic. At
times culture and nature can be contradictory, but not
on a journey such as this. My imagination and my
language were good tools for binding me closer to that
natural environment rather than distancing me from
it. I became a part of the ice, the snow and the wind
over the course of that journey, and that environment
gradually became part of me. Until then, most of my

life had revolved around valuing the big moments, not those considered small. Life as a consumer of products, but also feelings and time, is often about getting as much as possible out of a minimum of effort. On expeditions it is more about the opposite. On the ice and oceans, and in the mountains and forests, I learned that less can be more. I had to travel a long way before I realized that a little tastes a lot, less tastes more.

Perhaps thirty was rather late in the day to be coming to this realization. I remember as a child how a small piece of cake tasted better than a big piece, but I never drew any conclusions from that. Each new spoonful tasted less good than the one before, and if I ate enough I felt sick. That's what economists call the law of diminishing returns. Next time it was possible to eat a lot of cake I again ate as much as I could stuff down, naturally. But at times when there was only a small piece to be had, it meant I savoured it.

Now and then I still think it can be good to go the whole hog and dig in – but I'm glad I've become aware

of the pleasure of enjoying small helpings.
Architects, of course, made this discovery long ago.
'Less is more' is a principle attributed to the German
architect Mies van der Rohe. This might be a tad
unfair, considering all the time the expression was
familiar in architectural circles in Germany before it
was officially credited to him. He was, however, one
of those who really applied the consequences of this
philosophy, and in so doing became one of the
ground-breaking powers in modern architecture. He
showed that more of a good thing in architecture – as
elsewhere in life – doesn't necessarily reap the most
rewards. What is functional and beautiful in an
object should be revealed by the omission of certain
elements. Its strength as a whole will be increased by
using less of something. In architecture it isn't
always relevant to talk about the law of diminishing
returns. With buildings one tiny little excess really
can ruin the work.

In the Antarctic I had the freedom to choose what
I wanted at any time, much as at home. But unlike
life at home I was restricted to only a few options

from which to choose. When I wasn't on skis, I tried to do at least two things at the same time. To prepare lunch and fill Thermoses while I was reading and eating, and so forth. By and large all these duties were routine and on the list. There was nothing more to choose between or think about. All in all I was very efficient on the ice, and got done all I had to in the course of the day.

At home I value having the most possible choices at any given time, and being available almost all the time. To check the phone, help the kids with their homework, prepare food, evaluate projects – all more or less at the same time. The more I'm involved, the more I feel I'm getting out of life. From a logical viewpoint I can't see that that's a bad conclusion. The problem is that at times it can be limiting to have so many tasks at once, and so much to choose between. It's lovely to think of being faced with a choice of five different jams at breakfast, but it can also feel excessive and, therefore, wasteful. On expeditions I certainly didn't miss all the alternatives; I simply ate the same thing every day – oats, dried meat, chocolate with extra calories, honey, dried fruit, different sorts of fat, formula milk – and I felt I had earned my meals. The more exhausted I got, the better it tasted. If it was not too cold, I tried to read a little bit every evening. To save weight, the books I brought have as many thoughts and ideas as possible per gram. Later I recirculate the pages I have read as toilet paper.

The secret to a good life, seen from the ice, is to keep your joys simple. I don't see it as a goal to live as simply as this at home, but nor do I believe that the best thing for me is the maximum freedom of choice possible. It's always about having just enough options to feel I can choose one that works for me, but not so many that I feel I'm not able to assess the relative merits of each option. There's not as much difference as it appears between having no options and having a plethora of them. Both situations can render me powerless – although, on balance, I might prefer having no options to choose from. In that case I'm just frustrated, but if I have options and make the wrong choice, then I have frustration and regret to contend with.

*

On the eighth day of my journey to the South Pole, I discovered that the oatmeal soup tasted rancid. I was afraid of getting ill and had to throw it away. In my journal I recorded: 'I look down on the snow in front of me. The soup has filtered through the snow. The grains of oatmeal and the dried apricot are lying on top. Haven't the heart to let the apricots just lie there. I take off my right glove and pick them up, one by one. It's cold and laborious work. Stuff them into my mouth. Get my glove on. A bit of the sweet taste is left – I relish it.' I remember that taste even now, and how those apricots felt in my mouth, and I'm in no doubt that they're the best I've ever tasted.

I'm not going to tell my children that their lives will be better if they eat a couple of freezing apricots for breakfast. But I hope they won't grow up believing that life is most pleasurable when every meal is a feast. Or that it is worthwhile to sit indoors and live in images of the world rather than in the world. If they should ask me how they can balance the great and the small helpings in life, I won't have an inexhaustible supply of answers for them. You will not experience a golden mean for long, your goals may be different the next day, but it's good to strive for it nevertheless.

One Christmas, when my daughter Solveig was five, she turned to me after unwrapping her presents and said, 'Daddy, I have everything I need in life.' I remember thinking that our whole family had something to learn from Solveig that evening. Life feels richer when we adopt that outlook from time to time.

Now and again I dream about life on the ice, not just as a romantic or naive notion, but because I'm in no doubt whatsoever that life out there in all its simplicity was uncommonly rich. I felt I had everything I needed, and that I was the richest man in the whole world, even though I never thought about what I'd wear the next day – purely and simply because I had neither extra underwear nor extra outer garments.

*

11.
ACCEPT FAILURE

One of South America's foremost climbers, Rodrigo Jordan, told me that he has made 350 attempts to reach the summit of various mountains. About 120 of these attempts have been successful (of these, three were different routes up Everest). Those 230 other times he gave up. 'That's why I'm still alive,' he concluded.

I was positively surprised by his relaxed attitude to the failed attempts. Of course, I don't doubt that some of those had been, and continue to be, both demoralizing and embarrassing, but it's not often I meet someone who understands that success and failure aren't necessarily mutually exclusive. Quite the opposite; one is reliant upon the other, and both are a natural result of risking a little more. If one were never to fail, it would probably be because one didn't gamble sufficiently to start with. The view of the short-sighted would be that Rodrigo Jordan could have enjoyed many more successes if he hadn't given up so often, because he'd probably have got to the top of a good number of the mountains he hasn't managed to climb. Those with greater vision, on the other hand, would see that he'd almost certainly have suffered a serious accident, and in that sense a really significant failure. An accident that could have been fatal for himself and for those with whom he climbed.

When I was twenty-two, I believed I could make a real killing on the Stock Exchange. For a while I managed to finance my studies this way. Unfortunately for me, my self-confidence and the stakes rose faster than the level of my knowledge, and when the market crashed I lost most of what I had. I hadn't heard of a stop-loss. The most significant rule I failed to learn was this: you can't become too invested in your investments. Otherwise you'll fail to sell them while they're still valuable, and instead you'll be waiting till your shares have hit rock bottom before you're forced to get rid of them. When the market collapsed, I went into a cold sweat and fretted to such an extent I was in physical pain. Today I think back on that time as a very long day at school, where the curriculum consisted of learning humility and respect for the fact that not everything is easily achieved. I've learned more through failure than success. As Fridtjof Nansen said: experience is the best school but it's exceedingly expensive.

'Pain is temporary, quitting lasts for ever,' writes the cyclist Lance Armstrong, in his book *Every Second Counts*. I don't see things that way. Life is by its nature a constant stream of failures, small and large. I don't see my mistakes and losses as problems in themselves; it's the way in which I react to them which is decisive. Sometimes failure creates possibilities too. And failure is one of the most natural consequences of taking a little risk now and again.

The decathlon athlete Daley Thompson was asked what it was like to lose his world record without being able to regain it, and to go from being a hero to a 'has-been' overnight. I don't remember his precise response, but it was something akin to this: 'I took it like a real man, I cried for a week.' Thompson looked reality in the eye; he was no longer a sports star but a former sports star. He accepted it, was down for a week, then put it behind him. It's important to acknowledge, and by doing so expel, those feelings of grief when the world goes against you, rather than trying to keep a stiff upper lip. And then it's important not to allow those negative feelings to get the upper hand. Bitterness often arises when you don't accept life's realities. It's easy to remain miserable about what was or could have been and crawl into one's shell indefinitely, instead of searching for new possibilities on the horizon. And it's obviously easier to write about it than to do it.

Sackings, times of being passed over, divorces, financial losses, betrayal, the illness and death of loved ones – these are setbacks most of us experience at some point. Such things, of course, can be impossible to recover from. And yet, I think low times which don't also offer new possibilities are very much the exception. Now and again it's easy to forget that life – as a father, a publisher and an adventurer – is composed of a whole series of single episodes. My ability and will to respond to and absorb what happens to me are critical in deciding whether I weigh up that episode as positive or negative.

I don't know what the composer Beethoven (1770–1827) thought when he lost his hearing, or how the painter Goya (1746–1828) coped with the experience of gradually losing his ability to hear. Nor how Rembrandt (1606–69) coped with the death of his first wife or his later bankruptcy when his clients turned their backs on him. I love all three artists. But what I do know is that I consider the Ninth Symphony, which Beethoven composed after he had gone deaf, superior to most; and the paintings Rembrandt produced in the wake of his bankruptcy in 1656 to be superior to his early work – his brushstrokes became rougher and the colour incandescent. Had Goya stopped painting in 1790, when his hearing began to fail him, we'd never have seen any of the works for which he won such fame. His isolation from others and his failing hearing were seemingly a prerequisite for the conveying of his inner visions, thoughts and ideas onto canvas.

At times it can seem as though too few failures can weaken artistic development. If a writer's first book wins all sorts of major awards, it's often the case that the second book can be disappointing. A friend who has a gallery in Berlin told me that although he labours just as hard for the success of first-time exhibitors and the sale of all their work, in his heart of hearts he hopes it won't happen like that. Some sales are okay, but not too many. 'Overnight success doesn't do artistic talent a bit of good,' he maintains. Of course, he wishes the artist as a person all the luck in the world, but at the same time he knows their art will suffer if recognition comes too soon or too easily.

After becoming a publisher I've observed just how many mistakes I've made and yet still managed to run a healthy business. In the first years I fretted myself silly over all my failures. Good books that we mistakenly turned down, needless expenditures, bad judgement in respect of typescripts, covers and the sales potential of different books. One day I met up with another publisher and he told me that mistakes were part and parcel of every publisher's daily existence. It's basically impossible to run a business and not make mistakes. One's goal should be to not make the same mistakes again.

In Britain there's an expression I haven't encountered anywhere else – heroic failure. The manner in which one fails is decisive; if it's done in the way a Brit considers stylish, an amateurish but heroic attempt characterized by courage and backbreaking toil may be greater than the goal itself. In a land like Norway things are different – either we succeed or we fail. To speak of style in connection with this is outlandish. Have we gone too far in Norway, simply calling failure 'failure'? I think so. A failure can be many things. If, like Geir Randby, our companion to the North Pole, you slip a disc in your back when your sledge falls off an ice ridge, after two years of preparation and ten days in temperatures around minus 50, you are not to blame.

I still regret failures that I'm to blame for now and again. When I was younger I think I did so more frequently. I'm aware that more and more of those of my age have all but stopped doing so now, and have

begun instead to regret what they didn't do. Perhaps it wouldn't have been so silly after all to have attempted something exciting but risky earlier on in life. Perhaps when all is said and done, the mistakes and failures back then were some of our most formative experiences.

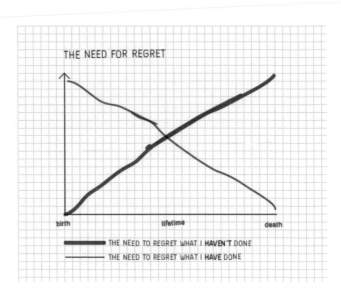

THE NEED FOR REGRET

birth   lifetime   death

THE NEED TO REGRET WHAT I **HAVEN'T** DONE
THE NEED TO REGRET WHAT I **HAVE** DONE

12.
FIND FREEDOM IN RESPONSIBILITY

When I was a small kid I dreamed now and again of living free from responsibilities and expectations. I wouldn't have to tidy my room or cut my hair, I'd have enough money and wouldn't go to school. When I was younger still, I even believed that life would be lovely as soon as I was wealthy enough to buy as many sweets as I wanted. Some years ago I saw that my own children, to a greater or lesser degree, were going through a similar phase. They were living in a Barbie economy where the most significant variable is how many Barbie dolls are available. Life without responsibility seemed the ultimate goal.

There's still a little voice inside that always tells me to take the easiest alternative. To go to see a film instead of visiting my family, to put off replying to messages, not to take responsibility for anyone but myself. A 'make-it-easy-for-myself' attitude. The Austrian psychiatrist Viktor E. Frankl (1905–97) survived several years in a Nazi concentration camp and said something about his experience which has stayed with me ever since I read it: 'Whoever has a why to live for, can bear almost any how.' We should not wish for less demanding lives, he writes in his 1946 book *Man's Search for Meaning*, for life has the potential to be meaningful under all manner of circumstances. Meaning comes from making the best of the situation in which we find ourselves.

That's not to say that we have to grin and bear every awful situation, nor that we can't allow ourselves to be miserable sometimes. I don't think it is in our nature as human beings to be content for long, our objectives are always changing and evolving along the way. No action or thought lasts as long as you want it to, wrote the nineteenth-century German poet Friedrich Hölderlin in his work *Hyperion*. 'That is the glory of man' – and by that he means his privilege, 'that nothing ever satisfies him'.

One of the reasons why I have dismissed the idea of living a life with few responsibilities is that I have realized responsibility is the key to a freer life. If I choose the path of least resistance, I am not free. If I avoid responsibility, I will always choose the easiest path when I come to any crossroad. In which case, my choices, both great and small, become predestined if I'm only looking for the easiest route. I am shackled by my own desire to be free.

What I once considered a free life (and still occasionally find appealing) – namely, doing as I pleased on each and every occasion, parties, studying, work, skiing, asking girls out at will – doesn't, in other words, appear so free after all. Now it mostly seems an arrogant way to live one's life. In a lecture to students at Kenyon College, Ohio, the American author David Foster Wallace talked about the importance of paying attention to what's happening right in front of you, rather than becoming preoccupied with abstract ideas. A free life should involve discipline, attention

and awareness, and, of course, generosity. Real freedom is being able 'to care about other people and to sacrifice for them, over and over, in myriad petty little unsexy ways, every day'. Reading those last seven words always makes me stop and think. The challenge, according to Wallace, is how to find meaning from your experience.

Responsibility and burdens give life substance. To choose only the easiest option is a recipe for emptying life of this substance. If your life doesn't make a difference to others, then in the long run it won't matter all that much to you either. Many people say that being able to choose the right course of action takes wisdom and experience. But I sometimes think we know a lot instinctively. It's the choosing that's the difficult part, no matter how old or wise we become.

As Foster Wallace told his students, taking up responsibility isn't always so easy, but: 'I wish you way more than luck.'

*

13.

MAKE FLEXIBILITY A HABIT

At the height of the IT wave at the end of the 1990s, the philosopher Lars Svendsen was asked to produce a report for one of Europe's leading telecommunications companies. His task was to investigate how habits were formed by the company's employees and how such habits could be broken. The company had just built a new head office and was keen to ensure that none of its employees would bring their old habits into the new workplace.

The problem for Svendsen was that he couldn't see how the firm could manage without routine. The formation of habit is a characteristic of creativity – 'Give the habits a good name,' was his conclusion.

Perhaps the company executive had read too much Immanuel Kant. Kant was crystal clear about the fact that it's important to prevent the formation of habit because habit denies us freedom and independence. Kant compares habit to a kind of constraint, in the sense that it becomes similar to a straitjacket from which one can't escape. Or maybe the executive was just following the advice he had read in some business book somewhere, who knows? But my own experience is that the more of my duties I manage to pack into routines, the more time I have left over to do other things and to think.

Kant was also, despite his avowed scepticism on the subject, a very real creature of habit himself, with an enormous capacity for work and creative production. The only thing I still remember about Kant from school is that the citizens of Königsberg – the city, now named Kaliningrad, where he lived all his life – could set their watches by his fixed daily walks.

One of history's least accessible philosophers, Georg W. F. Hegel, who to a considerable degree built his own theories on the works of Kant, described habit as our 'second nature' – meaning it was not quite an innate personality trait, but one that we turn to, almost automatically. He emphasized that this was something positive which human beings are reliant upon in order to live in a functional way.

When it comes to expeditions, it's my aim to nail as many duties as possible prior to departure, almost in a Hegelian manner. Of course, for me it's more about practicality than philosophy. There are so many decisions to be made in the course of a day in the mountains or on the ice that the fewer questions I have to deal with the better. As I've described before, I had to get up at the same time each day, and my morning routine had to be got through within a specific time. To achieve this, I had to do at least two things at once. For instance, while melting ice to drink I also had to carry out any necessary repairs on my equipment. And the very final thing I did each day after breaking camp was to turn and look around to see if I'd forgotten anything. That was vital, because to save weight I had hardly any spares, not even an extra pair of mittens, and I will never leave anything foreign

in the wilderness. This is a habit that will not die: every time I leave a table or room I automatically look around to see if I have forgotten something. After that, I walked for two hours, taking one break of ten minutes – and after nine of these minutes I got ready to walk again so I wouldn't lose time. I finished every day at a prearranged hour, and having set up camp I brushed off the snow and moisture from my clothes before crawling into the tent. After eating and some reading, I would lie down to sleep at the very same time each night.

Such a rigid structure may on the surface seem almost too pedantic and inflexible, but for me it laid the foundation for a good rhythm and inner tranquillity on the journey. When it's stormy, or when forty or fifty degrees of frost are crushing the body like wire-cutters, or when that same body is so exhausted it barely obeys orders, then it's absolutely vital to have a routine for support. In addition, having certain set patterns of behaviour allows you to enjoy moments when you act impulsively. Habit means that when I'm under pressure, when it's all but impossible to think clearly, I know what to do without thinking, because through force of that habit I've already established what actions to concentrate my energies on. I've found it helpful in my working life too, and when the kids were small and I had to endure endless sleepless nights with them. It's good to know that you're on top of the basics without having to think too much about them, especially when the going gets tough.

Of course, habits can have unfortunate consequences too. If followed too slavishly they can shut out a plethora of opportunities. And they can be taken to a comic extreme. There's a story told about one of the powerful Mexican earthquakes, this one from 1985, of a man who was found under the ruins of a house but who refused to crawl out. 'I can't because I've nothing on,' was his reasoning. Getting dressed was so ingrained in him that going out without clothes was completely unthinkable.

Out of curiosity, I've now and again imagined what would happen if a person became so defined by their habits that their personality ceased to exist. If they had become such a slave to routine and so predictable that they could quite simply be swapped in the workplace, in their circle of friends, and when at home with their partner and children – and no one would be any the wiser. Perhaps it was such an eventuality that bothered Kant, or Svendsen's taskmasters?

Alternatively, it's easy to imagine an individual who wants to do the opposite from everyone else at every given opportunity, to be unusual the whole time. To be so impulsive that they are never able to be punctual. The whole time this unusual individual must express just how 'out of the ordinary' they are. The irony is that I think that person will, despite their best efforts, end up resembling somebody conventional, almost to the extent that they too could be exchanged for someone else without anyone being aware of the swap, because, of course, this type of behaviour is a habit too.

The most exciting artists are almost all bound by routine, at least during those times when they're producing artistic work, though not quite to the extent that they live as I do prior to an expedition, with early mornings and a strict timetable. The stereotypical artist, the wine-swigging or drug-taking artistic soul who has no sense of work routine or adaptability whatsoever, exists too – but isn't as common as we are led to believe. And it's at least my experience that they seldom create great art during such periods of 'escape'. The Danish–Icelandic artist Olafur Eliasson generally arrives at his studio every day at the same time – half past eight in the morning. He does half an hour of archery to take his mind off everything else, before working solidly for the remainder of the day. The energy he saves by being systematic he employs in being creative.

Today, both in my life as a publisher and as the father of three children, I'm not as concerned with following set patterns as I was when on an expedition. Nonetheless, I'm convinced that even in a creative publishing firm, habit and routine are utterly necessary. Manuscripts have to be evaluated, worked on, tidied up and proofread at least twice after all the editorial work has been done. There's no point trying to do any jiggery-pokery, or finding some creative way round it. Agreements and deadlines have to be honoured. Our routines serve to create time for my colleagues and myself to be impulsive – to make surprising decisions, generate new ideas for books, and assess new opportunities. By doing so I achieve more joy for my colleagues as well as joy for myself as an employer and shareholder. This way, hopefully, the workplace is more fun than it might otherwise be.

And one aspect of habit that often gives me delight, and which people who constantly need to be spontaneous or unusual cannot enjoy, is that lovely feeling every now and then of simply not giving a damn about a habit when the moment feels right.

*

14.
DON'T LEAVE LUCK
TO CHANCE

From an objective standpoint I've generally been a physically weaker and less competent skier, sailor and mountaineer than many others. And no one believed I could ever manage to run a publishing house; many even continued to doubt it long after I'd started. Strictly speaking, I've only had two advantages over others with similar dreams: that I try hard and that I've been good at preparation – a bit better than some and a lot better than others. In that sense, I've had it easier en route. What I've lacked in terms of muscle and native wit I've tried to make up for by not standing about with my hands in my pockets.

'Victory awaits him who has everything in order – this is called good luck. For him who has neglected to take the necessary measures in time, failure is an absolute certainty – this is called bad luck.'

These words come from Roald Amundsen's account of how he became the first in history to reach the South Pole. Bold words, but accurate nonetheless. Amundsen only trusted his dogs and his men, while his competitors were less experienced and confident, and were hedging their bets using a combination of horses, motorized vehicles, dogs and man-hauling. How the day will turn out can be well and truly decided even before one leaves the tent in the morning. And probably before the expedition was even begun.

'If you make it, people will think you were lucky with the weather,' was the last thing the Norwegian artist Jakob Weidemann, our main sponsor for the expedition to the North Pole, said to Geir, Børge and myself before we left. I didn't think about his remark until after we'd come back from the pole and one person after another asked if we'd been lucky with the weather. Weidemann was a wise man. I am often asked if I have been lucky as an explorer.

Being lucky isn't about being more intelligent than other people or having special physical prowess. On the contrary, luck is about how we behave; what we think and feel. Of course, it's possible to have pure luck, to the extent that one attains something almost as a result of chance. Ringo Starr was a cool guy and a good drummer in the right place at the right time, for example. There's the story of a lottery winner who'd chosen the number forty-eight because for seven nights on the trot he'd dreamed of the number seven, and seven times seven is forty-eight, right . . . ? Well, no actually, but that's the number he gambled on.

But there's a big difference between the kind of luck one has once in a while and more systematic luck. It's the latter I'm interested in, because it is definitely possible to argue that not only Roald Amundsen but countless others like him were blessed with something resembling good luck. In the same way you could argue that great sailors have had luck with the wind. If we consider some of the global successes – photography, insulin, penicillin, the artificial production of nitrogen and the contraceptive pill – they're all seemingly the result of chance.

Ideally I should be prepared for every eventuality, but it's difficult to imagine that being possible. You can plan yourself to death. Conditions change, and my ability to respond to them is dependent on the time available to me along the way. Unforeseen and awkward circumstances will always arise, but the aim must be to limit them. If I'm successful in this respect, the chances are I'll have enough energy and resources to solve the challenges I haven't bargained for as and when they arise.

Simply deciding what to wear on my feet is a major task prior to setting out on each expedition. Warm feet, cool head, as a Norwegian expression goes. Amundsen called it 'the great goal' to come up with the perfect footwear solution. He spent two years designing and trying out boots before his expedition to the South Pole.

When I finally set off on an expedition, there's a certain satisfaction in knowing I've done everything I could have done beforehand. And more often than not, I feel like I'm attracting good fortune when I've done my homework. The possibilities pursue me. At other times I've been badly prepared. On those occasions it feels like I'm constantly on the defensive. Before I've solved one problem another has arisen. Then it feels as if bad luck is stalking me.

Before every expedition I've been on I have spent night after night sweating about my preparations. And although I probably worry more than is necessary, it's definitely better that way round. 'Be wary then; best safety lies in fear,' says *Hamlet*'s Laertes to his sister, Ophelia, as they are about to part. I think that's good advice to give someone you love.

If I grow too sure of myself, I become rather cocksure and not sufficiently self-critical. Then it's easy to overlook the small (or sometimes not so small) things that I should have noticed. All in all it's important to be a bit anxious – not only when making preparations – but until such time as the goal is reached. My experience is that most accidents happen on the way down from the mountains, when you feel happy and confident after having summited. As a publisher I've in no way reached any final objective, and I try all the time to take nothing for granted, and to sprinkle a moderate seasoning of worry into everyday activities. The day I begin to think that everything's under control will be the day my company has at least one problem . . . me.

Preparations are all about foreseeing difficulties. Alex Honnold tries to visualize all possibilities before he climbs because he does not want to climb halfway up and suddenly be surprised: '. . . Whoa, it never occurred to me that I would die if I fell here.' That is wise, but then once I'm underway I don't fear problematic situations until I actually encounter them. There's so much that can go wrong that it's just frustrating to worry about things beforehand. And more often than not the problem that crops up isn't the one I'd been fearing anyway. If I start fretting over every eventuality, knowing I can't do anything more to prevent them, then the chances are I'll start making excuses not to set off in the first place. And, as Ellen MacArthur, the British solo long-distance sailor, wisely explained: 'You don't fear for your life in the middle of a storm; you can't really afford to.'

For me, thinking positively is part of my preparations. I have a small but decisive bit of lore I actually think is completely self-taught; I've simply made up my mind not to think negatively about something once I've begun: 'This is something I'm going for. With heart and head, until it's proved undoable.' This applies as much to big things as to small. There are plenty of good reasons for swearing on an expedition, but doing so can all too easily encourage a negative frame of mind.

Sometimes I think we spend far too little time preparing for the important decisions in life, and yet we waste time in sweating the small ones. When in the late nineties my girlfriend and I decided to buy a place for our new family, I was surprised at the way otherwise level-headed individuals started making offers after being whisked once round a property. Buying a house is, for most of us, the biggest investment we'll make in life, but I have the

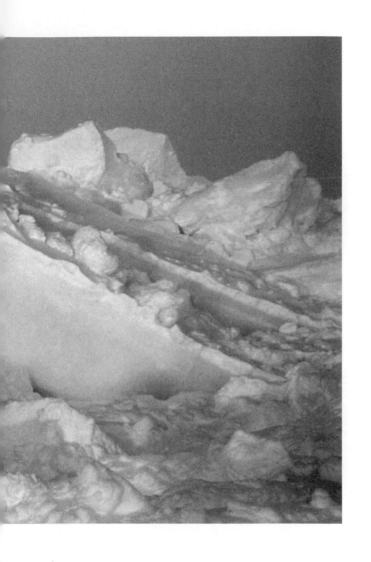

impression that only a few do anything other than rely on that first impression, the estate agent and the brochure. Not that first impressions aren't important, but I think it's not a bad idea to check to see whether there's damp in the basement.

Over the years many people have sought guidance on starting up a business, and still more have asked me for advice on planned expeditions. From the questions they ask I'm able to get a sense, fairly swiftly, of whether they'll have bad luck with the weather – or not – on the way. Much will be determined before they even set off. Of course, bad luck can befall anyone. You're hit with week after week of storms. There's a media strike the day you launch an important book. An apparently trustworthy individual breaks your trust and leaves you in the lurch. But my point is that difficult situations are always going to arise. The question is what you do before they hit. And how you react when they do.

*

15.

ALLOW YOUR GOAL TO PURSUE YOU

I quite often hear that the way to achieve your
goals is to imagine in great detail all the different
ways that success will affect your life. To write
down exactly why you're aiming for something.
Perhaps in some instances that works, but I am
inclined to think that's not always the best way.
Certainly when it comes to polar exploration, I don't
believe it's that simple. It is absurd to climb Everest,
just as it is absurd to walk to the poles, and that
makes it pretty difficult to fully explain the drive in
a rational way. As philosopher and mountaineer Arne
Næss replied when a journalist asked him why he had
started climbing: 'Why did you stop?'

The fact is that there's only rarely one single reason
for what we do. Some of our motives are very clear

before we start out on an expedition – curiosity, we were born to explore, love of nature, recognition (I didn't go to the South Pole in order to appear on the cover of the international edition of *Time* magazine, but my word was it gratifying to see myself there) – in fact they are what spur us to action; others often come to the fore only later. In my home life it's equally difficult to know whether I'm acting first out of love for the family, a sense of duty, my own interest or some other indefinable reason.

But while some motives aren't that easy to identify, or may be different according to each person's circumstances, I believe, from my own experience and from my encounters with others, that there are some motives which are behind almost every expedition. Out in the wide world those momentary flashes of experience can be compared to eternity. A few tenths of a second can feel like for ever. Past and future are meaningless when I cross a dangerous fissure in the ice, or for a second am captivated by some experience of the natural world. The split second and eternity need not be contradictory. Time is banished, and both things can be experienced at one and the same moment.

Such an experience may be a good reason to walk rather than drive, or to sail rather than fly over the ocean. It's enriching to decide to arrive somewhere under my own steam, and experience the journey over time, rather than just running to the fixed point. If the Oracle of Delphi had been contactable via phone in Ancient Greece, I still reckon people would have trudged up the slopes of Parnassus for answers to their questions. Going up the mountain is something else; to see the view and, in a way, feel that the heavens are parting as one nears the summit. I believe that most people who have gone climbing understand why the majority of the gods have their origins there.

The same need to know that I'm present in my own life drives me in the civilized world. I want to get the feeling that I'm mastering 'the game': the experience of freedom from something and to do something else, and that I myself have had a deciding influence on the result.

*

'Why walk alone to the South Pole instead of going by helicopter?' was never a question I asked myself before I did it. Explorers in general are more comfortable asking how, rather than why. For me it's always been a given that the former is more rewarding than the latter. The cold, the wind and all those steps are themselves a purpose.

I often think our real goals – the ones that guide and shape our lives – aren't ones that we ourselves actively pursue with pen, paper and a detailed five-year plan in hand. In my experience our real goals are the ones that are constantly there in the background. They might not be fully formed yet, and they might not make perfect sense, but we just can't seem to shake them. Those are the goals that seem to pursue us and they are, in my experience, the ones that have the most potential to change the course of our lives.

I spent the first decades of my life chasing different goals. When I was a kid I wanted to be like other kids. That was a goal in itself. I'd be as good at arguing as one, as rich as another, as good a footballer as a third, as handsome as a fourth and as likeable as a fifth. Five fine goals, but after a time I saw that I wasn't going to reach any of them. And that others wouldn't either, for that matter. It's one thing to have ideals, but it's another to dream of being like someone else. We humans are too different: simultaneously both you and the person you seek to emulate are changing – constantly. It's too easy to run away from oneself. I was chasing goals that weren't really mine, and therefore, like Heyerdahl's friends, I was never going to achieve them.

In my twenties I slowly started to see that my goals would eat me alive. I changed my focus and started to think about my background dreams, the ones that I had turned away from but which had never gone away. Becoming an explorer felt like I was following a predestined path.

*

As a child Roald Amundsen slept with his window wide open even through the bitter winter, preparing for being the first in history to walk to the North Pole. Then, in 1909, the American explorer Frederick Cook returned from the Arctic and claimed to have reached the pole in 1908. Soon after Cook's return another explorer from the US, Robert Peary, claimed it was him and not Cook who was the first. Amundsen was bitterly disappointed to have been beaten to his dream. But not for long. Soon the idea of walking to the South Pole came to him. He was already well prepared for the polar regions after all. He quite literally did a 180-degree turn. When, on 14 December 1911, he stood at the South Pole, he remarked drily: 'Never has any man stood so diametrically opposed from his desired destination.'

Mullah Nasruddin, the thirteenth-century satirist credited with bringing much humour and wisdom to Sufi culture, tells a different tale to Amundsen's. Once, a man found the mullah searching for something on the ground outside his house. When asked, Nasruddin replied that he was looking for his key. The man joined him in the search, but in due course asked the mullah: 'Where exactly did you drop this key?'

The mullah answered happily: 'Inside my house.'

'Then why on earth are you looking here?' the man asked, quite baffled.

'Because there is more light here than there is in my house,' replied the mullah.

Nasruddin is searching for the key in the wrong place – a bit like those who would love to be bestselling writers, but ignore the fact that they actually have to write a whole book first. Or those who want to become authors and insist on writing two books at the same time, meaning they never actually finish either. I've made this mistake a number of times myself, particularly as a teenager when I was making my first foray into the strange world of girls. I generally went straight in at the deep end, asked them out and was turned down. It took a lot of trial and error before it dawned on me that I might, first of all, have to make myself in some way attractive.

Likewise, to collect art, I first had to see a lot of art – moving, challenging, uncomfortable, seductive, funny, perverted, demanding and oddball art I quite often didn't understand. I spent years visiting galleries and museums. Then, having acquired some knowledge, I had to earn the money to buy it. I also had to read a great deal, get to know gallery owners and artists, and – eventually – reach a point where I started to understand what defines quality. It was a long haul. Quality art is much like a good novel: some things are said, others remain unsaid, and, in the end, some things remain unexplained. 'Rely on your own instincts when you buy art . . . and never compromise on quality' was the advice of the legendary Swiss art dealer Ernst Beyeler. Then, one day, you'll feel as if great art is chasing you, and not the other way round.

In his foreword to the seventy-third edition of *Man's Search for Meaning*, Viktor E. Frankl described how he wrote the book in nine consecutive days. To his surprise, the book became an instant bestseller. Perhaps it did so precisely because commercial success wasn't his aim first and foremost. He focused on writing a good and important work by his own standards, and not simply one that would appeal. As he himself stated: 'Success, like happiness, cannot be pursued.' The more you aim for success, the more likely you are to miss it. To Frankl, success was merely a side effect of his personal dedication to a greater

cause, and it pursued him because he 'had forgotten to think of it'.

Of course, there's no magic spell for achieving your goals, life-defining or otherwise. I don't always achieve mine. But I find it invariably helpful to reflect on past ambitions. Both the ones I didn't satisfy – when I was rejected by the girl I was keen on, almost sank in the Atlantic, failed as a speculator on the Stock Exchange, tried to earn money in the blink of an eye without first learning what such a feat required – and the ones I did. In theory, the recipe is pretty simple. On those occasions when I've jumped the fence at the highest point or taken a longer but richer route, the goal or goals have often come closer, almost of their own accord.

*

16.
RESET YOUR COMPASS

In 1985 Gary Kasparov won the best of twenty-four games against Anatoly Karpov to become the youngest chess champion ever. One of the first people he spoke to after his victory was Rona Petrosian, widow of the former world champion Tigran Petrosian.

'I'm sorry for you,' she said. 'Because the best day of your life is over.'

Kasparov had – thanks to his talent, purposeful training and an overprotective mother who kept him away from other temptations – achieved what had been his absolute goal in life, at the tender age of twenty-two. He expected to be nothing but overwhelmingly happy, but pretty quickly he was simply bewildered. Now what? What Kasparov basically needed was a new dream. He himself calls it 'champion's dilemma'. Chess is a sophisticated game:

after three opening moves there are nine million possible positions. But each and every life holds far more possibilities than a chessboard.

Magnus Carlsen became the world chess champion in 2013. Shortly before he won the title, my publishing house published a book about his career. During the writing of it I asked him how he would be able to keep up his motivation as more and more of his dreams were fulfilled. Carlsen didn't have a good answer. In March 2019, after several world championships, I asked him this same question. This time he had an answer. 'My motivation is to learn. I feel there are still so many things in chess that I don't know.' Interestingly he is wondering whether all the new knowledge will be an advantage: 'I don't know whether that will lead to playing better.' It can be too much knowledge. I get the impression that he finds it almost strange to think about how little he understood of the game six years earlier, when he became world champion for the first time.

The problem for many of my colleagues within the expedition world is that their ambition rests on the fulfilment of a single goal: of scaling a certain mountain or of reaching one particular place.

In that way they are a bit like Gary Kasparov, who thought only of becoming world champion, and they risk suffering from the same sense of loss that he did once they achieve it. I don't know just how many times I've heard tell of that emptiness experienced by adventure seekers once their goal has been reached. The excitement all the way and then the downward spiral once nothing remains to strive towards.

And I've experienced it myself. I remember what it was like to reach the South Pole and feel that I was standing at the end of the rainbow nearly forgetting my other dreams.

It became vital for me to reach new goals. The Norwegian philosopher Peter Wessel Zappfe wrote about something that could be called an explorer's dilemma. The life of an explorer has to end tragically: after the explorer has achieved something extraordinary, the public expect more, and the explorer is, at some point, either not able or willing to try. Soon after, they are forgotten, as was Roald

Amundsen after his great expeditions. Or the explorer tries to do something even more challenging than last time, and fails; or starts to cheat to make their accomplishments more impressive.

Mount Everest, the third pole, was my goal – to be the first to reach the world's three poles. I'm not saying that these expeditions were all about achievement for me. I believe that experiences of the natural world should be exactly that, and not about making or breaking records. On the other hand, I don't doubt that personal achievement is a big motivator for most explorers, though they often fail to mention it when they go on about peace, conservation, climate and cultural harmony. It's fairly clear to me, at any rate, that if I'd been concerned first and foremost with the view, one of the neighbouring peaks would have sufficed: much cheaper, less tiring and a better view by far. In addition to everything else, I would then have seen the world's highest mountain up close.

Once I'd climbed Everest I knew in my heart I had to keep thinking more expansively. I was on the point of completing all the adventures I had dreamed of . . . I knew I wouldn't stop going out on expeditions, but rather I'd cut down on all the trailing around, and for a while spend less time under the stars. What happened, almost of its own accord, was that all of a sudden I became a father for a first, a second and then a third time. It was a wonderful surprise. A dream fulfilled, and this in turn gave birth to innumerable new dreams and visions. Tongue in cheek, I've called my role as father 'the fourth pole'. It was certainly the easiest to reach, but by far the most demanding thereafter.

In the winter of 2004, I was in Copenhagen with a friend. One morning we walked across the city's Chambers Square. It was bitterly cold, and as usual at that hour there were some homeless folk standing huddled just beyond the railway station. One of these fellows came over to sell the Danish equivalent of *The Big Issue*, for which 50 per cent of the money goes to the person selling it. We all had plenty of time so we stood there talking. He was freezing cold and felt bitter towards a society he believed had failed him – but he still managed to be good-humoured. I, by contrast, didn't feel cheated by life – quite the opposite – but once again it struck me how alike we all are, even though we live such apparently different lives.

So I bought a copy of the paper this chap was selling. On the front page there was an article about dreams, about how difficult it can be to put them into words, and how vital it is to try nonetheless. The article described a survey in which many homeless addicts had been asked what dreams they had. Most said that they had no dreams whatsoever. I could see why someone in their position would feel like this. I have trouble defining my own dreams at times. But it was the last line of the article that has stayed with me ever since. *Oh yes you do have dreams. Please dream again.*

As an explorer I often think that nobody knows anything for sure. I don't know which peaks will suddenly appear before me that I'll choose – or be forced – to climb, or just decide to leave alone. I do think that having dreams, and wondering about the world around me, is what will keep me going, whichever route I take. And I'll try to stick to my own philosophy where I can, even though I slip up now and then, and will probably continue to do so. Of all the rules I've set myself over the years, there are two that I consistently try to stand by.

Firstly: be kind. Every day. Even on a solo expedition you are depending on dozens of others – the ones who make your boots, tent, sleeping bag and anorak, the nutritionist, sponsors – and kindness is met by helpfulness. To be nice is one of the most sensible things to be, and when your life may depend on those people, it is actually utterly stupid not to treat everybody well.

The second is an unwritten rule of the mountains and forests in Norway, namely that you should always leave the site of your camp as it was before you came, or in a better shape. I think that is the best rule we have in Norway. The only thing you should leave behind is a sense of gratitude. Gratitude for having had a break and for being on the move once again. The best things in life have no lasting forms. When you

move on, don't think too much. Look around you and up, into the sky – towards the sun, the moon, the stars – and listen to the surroundings: the rain falling, your foot rising from the wet moss and the silence. Ask yourself: where am I right now?

Thanks. I am here.

*

Notes

Foreword: Ground Yourself in Nature

Whittell, Giles, *Snow: The Biography* (Short Books Ltd, 2018)

3. Train Yourself in Optimism

Seligman, Martin, *Learned Optimism: How to Change Your Mind and Your Life* (New York: A. A. Knopf, 1990); the Zen stories may be found on various websites, including an article by the author Robert Heller: 'Commitment: Zen and the Art of Management'; the quote by Paul Vivek was in *Fortune* magazine, Europe Edition, 28 March, 2005

5. Don't Mistake Probability for Possibility

Berton, Pierre, *The Arctic Grail: The Quest for the North-West Passage and the North Pole, 1818–1909* (Viking, 1988); *Canada: Anchor Canada*, a book that includes the story of Polaris and https://en.wikipedia.org/wiki/Polaris_expedition; *Dogtown and Z-boys* (film, Columbia Tristar, 2001); Næss, Arne, *Hvor kommer virkeligheten fra? 18 samtaler med Arne Næss* (Oslo: Kagge Forlag, 2000); the information on Peter Benenson has been taken from his obituary in the *Economist*, Oslo, 5 March, 2005

6. Don't Take Stupid Risks

Miller, William Ian, *The Mystery of Courage* (London: Harvard University Press, 2000)

7. Have Something to Lose

Hugh Tredennick (ed.), Jonathan Barnes (introduction), J. A. K. Thomson (translator), Aristotle (Penguin Great Ideas, Penguin Books Ltd, 2004); *The Nicomachean Ethics* (Penguin Classics, 2004); Gillman, Peter (ed.), 'The Great

Mystery', by Tenzing Norgay, *Everest* (Little, Brown and Company, 2001); Nansen, Fridtjof, *Eventyrlyst*, editing and foreword by Erling Kagge (1942; Oslo: Kagge Forlag, 2011); Taylor, Charles, *Sources of the Self: The Making of the Modern Identity* (Cambridge: Cambridge University Press, 1989)

8. Don't Chase Happiness, Let It Chase You

The stories on Brooklyn and the family in Kamuli, Uganda, were originally published in Kagge, Erling, *Under Manhattan* (World Editions, 2015); Hugh Tredennick (ed.), Jonathan Barnes (introduction), J. A. K. Thomson (translator), Seneca, *On the Shortness of Life*, Aristotle (Penguin Great Ideas, Penguin Books Ltd, 2004); *The Nicomachean Ethics* (Penguin Classics, 2004); *The Cambridge Companion to Kant* (Cambridge: Cambridge University Press); Hamsun, Knut, *En vandrer spiller med sordin* (1909; Oslo: Gyldendal, 1993); *Science*, 3 December, 2004; Tomkins, Richard, *Financial Times*, 10 December, 2004; 'Either I'm happy, or I'm not, that's all', taken from a diary entry made on 8 July, 1916, cited in the 'Nachlass' manuscript, no. 103, p. 18r (8 July, 1916): Nachlass = Wittgenstein's works (1889–1951). The text was posthumously published in Ludwig Wittgenstein, *Notebooks/ Tagebücher 1914–1916*, edition H. von Wrightand, E. M. Anscombe (Suhrkamp 1960; Blackwell 1961) and later in 'Bergen Electronic Edition'. The story on Socrates and the relevance of pain I read in Montaigne, Michel de, *On Experience: The Complete Essays* (Penguin Classics, 1993); *Rolling Stone* magazine, 'Alex Honnold Documentary "Free Solo" is as Extreme as the Man', Peter Travers, 27 October, 2018; *Time* Magazine, 7 February, 2005, 'Lion's Roar: How Meditation Changes Your Brain – and Your Life', by Daniel Goleman and Richard Davidson, 7 May, 2018

9. Learn to be Alone

Hugh Tredennick (ed.), Jonathan Barnes (introduction), J. A. K. Thomson (translator), Aristotle (Penguin Great Ideas, Penguin Books Ltd, 2004); *The Nicomachean Ethics* (Penguin Classics, 2004); Svendsen, Lars, *A Philosophy of Boredom* (London: Reaktion Books Ltd, 1999, 2006)

10. Enjoy Small Helpings

Kant, Immanuel, '26: Of that estimation of the magnitude of natural things which is requisite for the Idea of the Sublime', *The Critique of Judgement* (Kessinger Publishing Co., 1790, 2004)

11. Accept Failure

Armstrong, Lance, *Every Second Counts* (USA: Vintage, 2004); Baylis, Nick, 'On the science of happiness', *The Times*, 18 December, 2004; Heller, Robert, and Carling, Will, *The Way to Win: Strategies for Success in Business and Sport* (Great Britain: Little, Brown and Company, 1995). The book has some amusing asides on Daley Thompson

12. Find Freedom in Responsibility

Frankl, E. Viktor, *Man's Search for Meaning* (London: Simon & Schuster, 1997). Frankl is furthering Friedrich Nietzsche and his well-known quote: 'He who has a why to live for can bear almost any how.' Hölderlin, Friedrich (1799; 1993): Hyperion, Philipp Reclam jun. verlag GmbH; https://www.1843magazine.com/story/david-foster-wallace-in-his-own-words

13. Make Flexibility a Habit

The Cambridge Companion to Kant (Cambridge: Cambridge University Press); I talked to Lars Svendsen about his experiences, spring 2004; I visited Olafur Eliasson in his studio in Berlin in 2004.

14. Don't Leave Luck to Chance

Amundsen, Roald, *Sydpolen. Den norske sydpolsferd med Fram 1910–1912* (1912; Oslo: Kagge Forlag, 2004); Shakespeare, William, *Hamlet* (Arden Edition of the Works of William Shakespeare), Jenkins (ed.); the story of the lottery winner was made up by Professor William Ziemba and cited in the *Financial Times* by Tim Harford: 'Resolving readers' dilemmas with the tools of Adam Smith'; *Spectator*, USA, Mary Wakefield: 'If I get an adrenaline rush, something's gone wrong', 7 February, 2019

15. Allow Your Goal to Pursue You

Coutu, Diane, 'l: Strategic intensity: a conversation with world chess champion Gary Kasparov', *Harvard Business Review*, April 2005; Frankl, E. Viktor, *Man's Search for Meaning* (London: Simon & Schuster, 1997); Marar, Ziyad, *Happiness Paradox* (London: Reaktion Books, 2004); books on Mulla Nasruddin by Idries Shah and various websites on Nasruddin; Christophe Mory, Ernst Beyeler, *A Passion for Art: Interviews*, Ernst Beyeler and Christophe Mory (authors), Isabel Feder (translator), Sam Keller (foreword), (Hardcover, 2011; Scheidegger and Spiess, revised edition, 2011)

16. Reset Your Compass

Zapffe, Peter Wessel, *Kvalificerede katastrofer bestemmelse av det objektivt tragiske, Om det tragiske* (1941; Oslo: Pax Forlag, 1996). To always leave the site of your camp as it was before you rested and to feel gratitude is not only a Norwegian idea. According to French author Sylvain Tesson in his book *Constellations of the Forest* (USA: Rizzoli Ex Libris, 2013), Robert Baden-Powell's similar advice was: 'When through with a campsite, take care to leave two things behind. Firstly: nothing. Secondly: your thanks.' I have searched but not seen this quote in other places. Tesson suggests it should be made a universal principle. A very good idea

My own books have also been used as source material in several of the chapters.

Kagge, Erling, *Nordpolen: Det Siste Kappløpet* (Oslo: Cappelen, 1990)
— , *Alone to the South Pole* (Oslo: Cappelen, 1993)
— , *Under Manhattan* (World Editions, 2015)
— , *Silence: In the Age of Noise* (Viking, 2017)
— , *Walking: One Step at a Time* (Viking, 2019)

Acknowledgements

Thanks to Rosanna Forte, Joakim Botten, Petter Skavlan, Gabi Gleichmann, Nick Baylis, Kristin Brandtsegg Johansen, Lars Svendsen, Morten A. Strøksnes, Nina Ryland, Unni Lindell, Knut Olav Åmås, Astrid de Vibe, Lars Lenth, Espen Røysamb, Guro Solberg, Mark Handsley, Yonca Dervisoglu and the late Arne Næss for commenting so generously on the text; all twenty-six colleagues at Kagge Forlag; Mary Mount, Venetia Butterfield, Ellie Smith and Olivia Mead at Viking Penguin; Hans Petter Bakketeig at Stilton Literary Agency and Annabel Merullo at Peters, Fraser and Dunlop; and my family.

Thanks also to my friends from my many expeditions – crossing the Atlantic Ocean in *Jeanette IV* in 1983 and 1984: Hauk Wahl, Morten Stødle (Morten was injured so couldn't make the return voyage) and Arne Saugstad; going to the North Pole in 1990: Geir Randby (Geir suffered a slipped disc after ten days and had to give up) and Børge Ousland; climbing Everest in 1994: Ang Dorje, Nima Gombu, Norbu, David Keaton,

Hall Wendel, David Taylor, Ekke Gundelach, Hellmut Seitzl, Kami Tenzing Sherpa (he helped me a lot before the journey), Ed Viesturs and the inimitable Rob Hall, who passed away peacefully just below the summit of Everest in May 1996; crossing Vatnajökull in Iceland in 2010: Haraldur Örn Olafsson and Børge; and walking in New York City with Steve Duncan plus friends who joined for parts of our journey.

Images

Many of the photographs in this book are
my own, taken on the expeditions I discuss in its
pages. I am otherwise very grateful to fellow
adventurers for allowing me to use their photographs:
Børge Ousland for the images on pages viii–ix, 36,
58–9, 79, 113, 128–9, 144–5, 158 and 170–71; Kjell Ove
Storvik for the images on pages x–xi, 70, 93, 168–9;
Rob Hall for the image on page 65; David Keaton for
the images on pages 43 and 155; Haraldur Örn
Ólafsson for the image on page xvii; and Lars Ebbesen
for the illustrations on pages 17 and 118. Plus the
Grenna Museum for the images of Salomon August
Andrée's expedition on pages 52–4; NASA Image
Collection / Alamy Stock Photo for the image of the
Kon-Tiki raft on page 5; Ceal Floyer and Esther
Schipper for the reproduction of Ceal Floyer's *Snow
Globe* (2017, edition 11/30), photo © Andrea Rossetti on
page v.